HOW TO START A CAR DEALERSHIP

Introduction: Welcome to Your Guide on Managing a Successful Car Dealership

Welcome to this comprehensive guide designed to equip you with the knowledge and strategies necessary to thrive in the dynamic world of automotive dealership management. Whether you're embarking on a new venture or seeking to enhance your existing dealership's operations, this book is tailored to provide practical insights and actionable steps to drive your success.

Throughout these chapters, we'll explore every facet of dealership management, from laying a strong foundation with effective business planning and financial management to implementing robust marketing strategies, delivering exceptional customer service, fostering strong leadership, and optimizing operational efficiency. Each topic is crafted with the goal of helping you build a resilient and customer-focused dealership that stands out in the competitive automotive market.

Drawing from industry best practices and real-world examples, this guide offers not only theoretical knowledge but also practical advice that you can immediately apply to your dealership operations. Whether you're looking to refine your sales techniques, improve inventory management, leverage digital marketing, or enhance customer satisfaction, you'll find valuable insights to guide your decisions and actions.

By the end of this journey, my aim is for you to feel empowered with the tools and strategies needed to navigate challenges, capitalize on opportunities, and achieve sustainable growth for your automotive dealership. Let's embark on this journey together, as we pave the road to your dealership's success.

Here's to a prosperous future in the automotive industry!

Copyright © 2024

All rights reserved. No part of this book may be reproduced in any form or by any electronic or mechanical means, including information storage and retrieval systems, without permission in writing from the publisher, except by a reviewer, who may quote brief passages in a review.

The information contained in this book is for general information purposes only. The information is provided by naciro and while we endeavor to keep the information up to date and correct, we make no representations or warranties of any kind, express or implied, about the completeness, accuracy, reliability, suitability or availability with respect to the book or the information, products, services, or related graphics contained in the book for any purpose. Any reliance you place on such information is therefore strictly at your own risk.

All trademarks and registered trademarks are the property of their respective owners and are used in this book only for identification and explanation.

Permission to use copyrighted material in this book should be obtained from the copyright owner or the publisher.

This book is not intended to provide medical, legal, or financial advice, and the author and publisher specifically disclaim any liability for any loss or damage caused or alleged to be caused directly or indirectly by the information in this book.

Naciro and the publisher of this book do not endorse or recommend any commercial products, processes, or services. The views and opinions of authors expressed in this book do not necessarily state or reflect those of the publisher of this book.

Contents

Chapter 1: Introduction to the Car Dealership Industry

Chapter 2: Market Research and Feasibility Study

Chapter 3: Business Planning and Strategy

Chapter 4: Legal Requirements and Regulations

Chapter 5: Location and Facilities

Chapter 6: Financing and Funding Your Dealership

Chapter 7: Inventory Management Strategies

Chapter 8: Sales Techniques and Customer Engagement

Chapter 9: Service Department Operations and Customer Satisfaction

Chapter 10: Marketing Strategies for Your Car Dealership

Chapter 11: Customer Service Excellence

Chapter 12: Staff Development and Team Building

Chapter 13: Operational Efficiency and Process Optimization

Chapter 14: Financial Management for Your Car Dealership

Chapter 15: Community Engagement and Building Relationships

Chapter 16: Innovation in Automotive Retail

Chapter 17: Marketing Strategies for Automotive Dealerships

Chapter 18: Customer Service Excellence

Chapter 19: Effective Inventory Management

Chapter 20: Financial Management for Automotive Dealerships

Chapter 21: Leadership Principles for Automotive Dealerships

Chapter 22: Achieving Operational Excellence in Your Car Dealership

Chapter 23: Marketing Strategies for Automotive Dealerships

Chapter 24: Customer Service Strategies for Automotive Dealerships

Chapter 25: Financial Management for Automotive Dealerships

Chapter 26: Leadership Principles for Automotive Dealerships

Chapter 27: Digital Marketing Strategies for Automotive Dealerships

Chapter 28: Inventory Management Strategies for Automotive Dealerships

Chapter 29: Customer Service Excellence in Automotive Dealerships

Chapter 1: Introduction to the Car Dealership Industry

Welcome to the exciting world of car dealerships! Whether you're a seasoned entrepreneur or someone looking to dive into the automotive retail business for the first time, understanding the dynamics of this industry is crucial for success.

The Automotive Retail Sector: A Snapshot

Imagine a bustling showroom with sleek vehicles, customers eagerly exploring their options, and a team of sales professionals ready to assist. This is the heartbeat of a car dealership—an environment where buying a car isn't just a transaction but an experience.

The Role of Car Dealerships

Car dealerships play a pivotal role in the automotive ecosystem. Beyond just selling vehicles, they serve as hubs for vehicle servicing, financing, and customer support. Dealerships bridge the gap between automotive manufacturers and consumers, offering a personalized touch that online marketplaces often lack.

Trends and Transformations

In recent years, the automotive retail sector has undergone significant transformations. Technological advancements have reshaped how dealerships operate, from digital showrooms to online sales platforms. The rise of electric vehicles (EVs) and sustainable practices has also influenced consumer preferences, challenging dealerships to adapt their offerings and services.

Challenges and Opportunities

Like any industry, car dealerships face their share of challenges. Competition is fierce, customer expectations are higher than ever, and regulatory requirements can be complex. However, these challenges also present opportunities for innovation and differentiation.

Successful dealerships leverage technology to streamline operations, focus on customer experience to build loyalty, and stay ahead of industry trends to capitalize on emerging markets.

Why Choose Car Dealership Business?

Entrepreneurial Freedom

Running a car dealership offers entrepreneurial freedom. You have the flexibility to set your own business model, choose the brands you want to represent, and create a unique identity within your community.

Potential for Profitability

The automotive retail industry is known for its potential profitability. While profit margins on vehicle sales can vary, dealerships often generate revenue from financing, service contracts, parts sales, and aftermarket accessories.

Serving Your Community

A dealership isn't just a business—it's a cornerstone of the community. You become a trusted advisor for customers seeking reliable transportation, a local employer providing jobs, and a contributor to community events and sponsorships.

Conclusion

Starting a car dealership is more than a business venture; it's a commitment to providing exceptional service, building lasting relationships, and staying at the forefront of an evolving industry. Throughout this guide, we'll explore every aspect of launching and managing a successful dealership, empowering you with the knowledge and tools to thrive in this dynamic marketplace. Whether you're inspired by innovation, driven by profitability, or motivated by community impact, the journey starts here.

Chapter 2: Market Research and Feasibility Study

Before embarking on the exciting journey of starting a car dealership, it's essential to lay a solid foundation through thorough market research and a feasibility study. This chapter will guide you through the process of understanding your target market, analyzing competition, and assessing the viability of your dealership business idea.

Understanding Your Target Market

The success of any car dealership hinges on understanding and catering to the needs of your target market. Here's how you can effectively research and define your customer base:

Demographic Analysis

Start by identifying the demographic profile of potential customers. Consider factors such as age, income level, occupation, family size, and lifestyle preferences. Understanding who your customers are will help you tailor your inventory, pricing strategies, and marketing efforts accordingly.

Geographic Considerations

Evaluate the geographic area you plan to serve. Is it urban, suburban, or rural? What are the transportation needs and preferences of residents in this area? Geographic analysis will influence your dealership location, inventory mix, and marketing approach.

Psychographic Insights

Delve into the psychographics of your target market—their attitudes, values, interests, and lifestyle choices. Are they eco-conscious and interested in electric vehicles? Do they prioritize safety features or luxury amenities? Psychographic insights will guide your inventory selection and customer engagement strategies.

Analyzing the Competition

Competitive analysis is crucial for positioning your dealership effectively within the marketplace:

Identify Direct Competitors

Research existing car dealerships in your area and beyond. Identify their strengths, weaknesses, pricing strategies, customer service approaches, and market share. Understanding your competitors' offerings will help you differentiate your dealership and carve out a unique selling proposition (USP).

SWOT Analysis

Conduct a SWOT (Strengths, Weaknesses, Opportunities, Threats) analysis for your dealership and competitors. Assess internal factors like your dealership's location, expertise, and financial resources, as well as external factors such as economic trends, regulatory changes, and technological advancements.

Feasibility Study: Assessing Viability

A feasibility study is a critical step to evaluate the financial and operational feasibility of your car dealership business idea:

Financial Projections

Estimate your startup costs, ongoing expenses, and revenue projections. Consider expenses such as leasing or purchasing dealership space, inventory acquisition, staffing costs, marketing expenses, and regulatory fees. Develop a comprehensive financial plan to ensure your dealership can achieve profitability.

Demand Analysis

Evaluate the demand for vehicles in your target market. Consider factors such as population growth, consumer preferences, economic conditions, and industry trends. Assess whether there is sufficient demand to support your dealership's sales goals and revenue projections.

Operational Considerations

Outline the operational requirements of your dealership, including staffing needs, inventory management systems, customer service protocols, and compliance with regulatory requirements. Identify potential operational challenges and develop strategies to mitigate risks.

Conducting Market Research

Primary Research

Engage directly with potential customers through surveys, focus groups, and interviews to gather insights into their buying preferences, expectations, and pain points. Primary research provides firsthand data to inform your dealership's strategy.

Secondary Research

Utilize secondary sources such as industry reports, demographic data, and market analyses to supplement your primary research findings. Secondary research offers valuable context and benchmarks for understanding market trends and competitive dynamics.

Conclusion

Market research and a feasibility study are foundational steps in launching a successful car dealership. By understanding your target market, analyzing competitors, and assessing the viability of your business idea, you'll be equipped with the knowledge and insights to make informed decisions throughout your entrepreneurial journey.

Stay tuned as we explore further chapters on business planning, legal considerations, financing options, and more, all designed to support you in building a thriving dealership business.

Chapter 3: Business Planning and Strategy

Congratulations on taking the next step toward launching your car dealership! A well-crafted business plan and strategic vision are essential to navigate the complexities of the automotive retail industry. In this chapter, we'll explore how to develop a comprehensive business plan, define your dealership's strategic direction, and set the foundation for long-term success.

Crafting Your Business Plan

A business plan serves as the roadmap for your dealership, outlining your goals, strategies, and operational details. Here's how to create a robust business plan:

Executive Summary

Start with an executive summary that provides an overview of your dealership's mission, vision, and key objectives. Highlight the unique aspects of your business, target market insights, and your competitive advantage.

Business Description

Describe your dealership's business model, including the types of vehicles you'll sell (new, used, luxury, etc.), your market niche, and the geographic area you'll serve. Outline your dealership's legal structure (sole proprietorship, partnership, LLC, etc.) and location details.

Market Analysis

Summarize your market research findings from Chapter 2. Detail your target market demographics, psychographics, and geographic considerations. Analyze industry trends, customer preferences, and competitive dynamics that will impact your dealership.

Organization and Management

Introduce your dealership's organizational structure and management team. Highlight key personnel roles, their qualifications, and their responsibilities. Outline your hiring plan and any partnerships or advisory relationships.

Product Line and Services

Detail the vehicles and services your dealership will offer. Include information on your inventory strategy, pricing models, financing options, warranties, service department offerings, and aftermarket products.

Sales and Marketing Strategy

Outline your sales approach and marketing strategies to attract and retain customers. Include your promotional tactics, digital marketing plans, advertising channels, and customer relationship management (CRM) strategies.

Financial Projections

Present detailed financial projections for your dealership. Include startup costs, monthly expenses (e.g., rent, salaries, inventory), revenue forecasts, cash flow projections, and break-even analysis. Use realistic assumptions based on your market research and industry benchmarks.

Funding Requirements

Specify your funding needs to launch and sustain your dealership until profitability. Detail how much capital you require, how you'll use the funds (e.g., inventory purchase, marketing, facility improvements), and your financing options (e.g., loans, investors, personal savings).

Appendices

Include supporting documents such as resumes of key team members, lease agreements, market research data, supplier agreements, and any legal documents pertinent to your dealership's operations.

Defining Your Strategic Direction

A clear strategic direction will guide your dealership's growth and sustainability:

Mission and Vision Statements

Craft a compelling mission statement that encapsulates the purpose and values of your dealership. Define a visionary statement that articulates your long-term aspirations and goals.

SWOT Analysis

Referencing your SWOT analysis from Chapter 2, identify strategic initiatives to leverage strengths, mitigate weaknesses, capitalize on opportunities, and navigate potential threats.

Competitive Advantage

Articulate your dealership's unique selling proposition (USP) based on factors such as superior customer service, exclusive product offerings, pricing advantages, or specialized expertise.

Growth Strategies

Outline strategies for expanding your dealership's market share, enhancing customer retention, and exploring new revenue streams. Consider avenues such as online sales, additional service offerings, or geographic expansion.

Conclusion

Crafting a comprehensive business plan and defining your dealership's strategic direction are pivotal steps toward building a successful automotive retail business. Your business plan serves as a blueprint for achieving your goals, securing financing, and aligning your team's efforts. Stay tuned as we delve into subsequent chapters on legal requirements, financing options, location considerations, and operational essentials, all aimed at empowering you to launch and manage a thriving car dealership.

Chapter 4: Legal Requirements and Regulations

Welcome to Chapter 4 of your journey to starting a car dealership! Navigating the legal landscape is crucial to ensuring your dealership operates smoothly and complies with all necessary regulations. In this chapter, we'll explore the essential legal requirements you need to consider when establishing your car dealership business.

Registering Your Business

The first step in establishing your car dealership is to choose a legal structure and register your business:

Legal Structure Options

Consider options such as sole proprietorship, partnership, limited liability company (LLC), or corporation. Each structure has different implications for liability, taxes, and operational flexibility. Consult with a legal advisor or accountant to determine the best fit for your dealership.

Registering Your Business Name

Choose a unique and memorable name for your dealership that reflects your brand identity. Check availability and register your business name with the appropriate state or local authorities. Ensure it complies with naming regulations and trademarks.

Obtaining Licenses and Permits

Car dealerships are heavily regulated and require various licenses and permits to operate legally:

- **Dealer License**: Obtain a dealer license from your state's Department of Motor Vehicles (DMV) or regulatory agency. Requirements vary by state and may include background checks, bonding, and completion of a dealer training program.

- **Sales Tax Permit**: Register for a sales tax permit with your state's tax authority to collect sales tax on vehicle sales and services.
- **Zoning Permits**: Ensure your dealership location complies with local zoning laws and obtain any necessary permits for commercial use.
- **Environmental Permits**: Depending on your location and activities, you may need permits related to environmental regulations, waste disposal, or hazardous materials handling.

Compliance with Federal Regulations

Understand and comply with federal regulations that impact car dealerships:

- **Federal Trade Commission (FTC)**: Adhere to regulations concerning consumer protection, advertising practices, and the sale of used vehicles under the Used Car Rule.
- **Environmental Protection Agency (EPA)**: Comply with emissions standards and regulations, especially if you service vehicles or handle refrigerants.
- **Occupational Safety and Health Administration (OSHA)**: Ensure workplace safety compliance for dealership employees.

Contracts and Legal Agreements

Purchase and Sales Agreements

Develop standard purchase and sales agreements that outline terms of vehicle sales, warranties, and customer obligations. Ensure agreements comply with state laws governing vehicle sales and consumer protection.

Financing and Leasing Contracts

If offering financing or leasing options, establish legal contracts that disclose terms, interest rates, repayment schedules, and consumer rights under the Truth in Lending Act (TILA) and other finance regulations.

Employment Contracts and Policies

Create employment contracts outlining job responsibilities, compensation, benefits, and termination procedures. Develop employee handbooks that communicate workplace policies, codes of conduct, and anti-discrimination policies.

Insurance Coverage

Dealership Insurance

Protect your dealership against risks with comprehensive insurance coverage:

- **General Liability Insurance**: Covers bodily injury, property damage, and legal expenses arising from dealership operations.
- **Garage Liability Insurance**: Protects against liabilities related to test drives, customer vehicles in your care, and dealership premises.
- **Inventory Insurance**: Insures vehicles against theft, damage, or loss while in your dealership's possession.
- **Worker's Compensation Insurance**: Provides coverage for employee injuries and medical expenses.

Document Retention and Compliance

Maintain accurate records and documentation to demonstrate compliance with legal requirements:

- **Vehicle Titles and Registration**: Keep records of vehicle titles, registrations, and transfers to ensure compliance with state DMV regulations.

- **Financial Records**: Maintain financial records, including sales transactions, taxes collected, and expenditures, for auditing and tax filing purposes.

Conclusion

Understanding and complying with legal requirements is essential for the successful launch and operation of your car dealership. By securing the necessary licenses, drafting legal agreements, obtaining adequate insurance coverage, and maintaining compliance with federal and state regulations, you can mitigate risks and build a solid foundation for your dealership's future. In the next chapters, we'll delve into financing options, location considerations, inventory management, and marketing strategies—all designed to support your journey toward establishing a thriving automotive retail business.

Chapter 5: Location and Facilities

Welcome to Chapter 5 of your guide on starting a car dealership! Choosing the right location and designing functional facilities are crucial steps in establishing a successful dealership. This chapter will explore how to select an optimal location, design an inviting showroom, and ensure your dealership's facilities support efficient operations and exceptional customer experiences.

Choosing the Ideal Location

The location of your dealership can significantly impact its success. Consider the following factors when selecting a location:

Accessibility and Visibility

Choose a location that is easily accessible to your target market and visible from major roads or highways. High visibility increases foot traffic and attracts potential customers passing by.

Demographics and Market Area

Evaluate the demographics of the surrounding area to ensure it aligns with your target customer profile. Consider population density, income levels, consumer preferences, and transportation needs. A location near residential neighborhoods or commercial hubs can enhance customer reach.

Competition and Market Saturation

Assess the presence of competitors in the area. While some competition can indicate a viable market, too many dealerships offering similar products may increase competition for customers. Consider how your dealership can differentiate itself in a competitive market.

Zoning and Regulatory Compliance

Verify that the location complies with local zoning regulations for commercial use. Obtain any necessary permits or approvals from local authorities before finalizing the lease or purchase agreement.

Designing Your Dealership Facilities

Creating a functional and appealing dealership environment is essential for customer engagement and operational efficiency:

Showroom Layout and Design

Design a showroom that showcases vehicles effectively and provides a welcoming atmosphere for customers. Consider factors such as lighting, flooring, signage, and comfortable seating areas for customer consultations.

Service Department Setup

If offering vehicle servicing, design a service department that maximizes efficiency and customer satisfaction:

- **Service Bays**: Determine the number of service bays needed based on anticipated demand and service volume.
- **Equipment and Tools**: Equip service bays with the necessary tools, diagnostic equipment, and lifts to facilitate efficient repairs and maintenance.
- **Customer Amenities**: Provide amenities such as a customer waiting area with comfortable seating, refreshments, Wi-Fi access, and transparent viewing of service work.

Parts and Accessories Display

Create a dedicated area for displaying parts, accessories, and aftermarket products. Organize displays in a way that encourages upselling and showcases the range of products available to customers.

Facility Considerations

Parking and Vehicle Storage

Ensure ample parking space for customers and employees. Designate areas for vehicle display, test drives, and customer parking to accommodate peak traffic periods.

Security and Safety Measures

Implement robust security measures to protect dealership assets, vehicles, and customer information:

- **Surveillance Systems**: Install CCTV cameras and alarm systems to monitor dealership premises and deter theft.
- **Access Control**: Restrict access to sensitive areas such as vehicle storage lots and administrative offices.
- **Safety Protocols**: Implement safety protocols for handling vehicles, hazardous materials, and emergency situations.

Lease vs. Purchase Considerations

Decide whether to lease or purchase dealership facilities based on your financial resources and long-term business goals:

- **Leasing**: Leasing offers flexibility with lower initial costs and the ability to relocate easily if needed. Negotiate lease terms that align with your dealership's growth plans and budget constraints.
- **Purchasing**: Purchasing property provides long-term stability and potential appreciation in property value. Evaluate financing options and consider the impact on cash flow and operational expenses.

Conclusion

Choosing an optimal location and designing functional facilities are critical decisions that shape the success of your car dealership. By considering factors such as accessibility, demographic alignment, competition, zoning regulations, and facility design, you can create a dealership environment that attracts customers, supports operational efficiency, and enhances overall customer satisfaction. In the next chapters, we'll explore inventory management strategies, financing options, staffing considerations, and marketing tactics—all essential components for building and growing a thriving automotive retail business.

Chapter 6: Financing and Funding Your Dealership

Welcome to Chapter 6 of your comprehensive guide on starting a car dealership! Securing financing and funding is a crucial step in turning your business idea into reality. In this chapter, we'll explore various financing options, budgeting considerations, and strategies to manage cash flow effectively for your dealership.

Estimating Startup Costs

Before seeking financing, it's essential to estimate the startup costs required to launch your car dealership:

Initial Expenses

- **Inventory**: Estimate the cost of acquiring initial vehicle inventory, including new and used vehicles. Consider factors such as make, model, and market demand.
- **Facilities**: Calculate expenses for leasing or purchasing dealership space, facility renovations, signage, and showroom setup.
- **Equipment**: Budget for essential equipment and tools needed for vehicle servicing, parts storage, and showroom displays.
- **Legal and Licensing Fees**: Include costs for obtaining dealership licenses, permits, legal consultations, and compliance with regulatory requirements.

Operational Expenses

- **Personnel**: Estimate payroll expenses for hiring dealership staff, including salespeople, service technicians, administrative personnel, and management.
- **Marketing and Advertising**: Allocate funds for initial marketing campaigns, digital advertising, print materials, and promotional events to attract customers.

- **Insurance**: Budget for various insurance policies, including liability insurance, dealership inventory insurance, worker's compensation, and property insurance.

Financing Options for Dealerships

Traditional Bank Loans

- **Term Loans**: Secure a term loan from a bank or financial institution to finance startup costs or ongoing operational expenses. Repayment terms, interest rates, and loan amounts vary based on creditworthiness and collateral.
- **Lines of Credit**: Access a revolving line of credit to manage cash flow fluctuations, cover short-term expenses, or seize business opportunities as they arise.

SBA Loans

- **Small Business Administration (SBA) Loans**: Explore SBA loan programs designed to support small businesses, including dealership startups. SBA loans offer competitive terms and lower down payments compared to conventional loans.

Dealer Floor Plan Financing

- **Floor Plan Financing**: Obtain financing specifically for purchasing vehicle inventory. Dealership floor plan loans allow you to borrow against vehicles in inventory and repay the loan as vehicles are sold.

Manufacturer Financing Programs

- **Manufacturer Financing**: Partner with automotive manufacturers offering financing programs to support dealership startups. These programs may include vehicle incentives, financing terms, and promotional support.

Private Investors and Partnerships

- **Angel Investors and Venture Capital**: Seek funding from private investors or venture capital firms interested in automotive retail ventures. Prepare a compelling business plan and pitch to attract potential investors.

Personal Savings and Equity

- **Personal Savings**: Invest personal savings or equity from business partners to fund startup costs and initial operations. Consider the impact on personal finances and risk tolerance.

Budgeting and Cash Flow Management

Creating a Budget

- **Budget Development**: Develop a detailed budget outlining anticipated revenues and expenses for the first year of operations. Include contingencies for unexpected costs or fluctuations in market conditions.
- **Monitoring Expenses**: Monitor expenses closely and identify opportunities to reduce costs without compromising service quality or customer experience.

Cash Flow Management

- **Cash Flow Forecasting**: Forecast cash flow projections to anticipate revenue cycles, inventory turnover, and operating expenses. Maintain adequate cash reserves to cover operational costs and unexpected expenses.
- **Inventory Management**: Implement efficient inventory management practices to optimize cash flow, minimize carrying costs, and ensure vehicles are sold within a reasonable timeframe.

Conclusion

Securing financing and effectively managing cash flow are critical components of launching and sustaining a successful car dealership. By estimating startup costs, exploring financing options tailored to dealership needs, creating a realistic budget, and implementing sound cash flow management strategies, you can position your dealership for growth and profitability. In the next chapters, we'll delve into inventory sourcing, sales strategies, customer relations, and operational excellence—all essential elements for building a thriving automotive retail business.

Chapter 7: Inventory Management Strategies

Welcome to Chapter 7 of your guide on starting a car dealership! Effectively managing your inventory is crucial to the success of your dealership. This chapter will explore proven strategies for sourcing, stocking, and selling vehicles to maximize profitability and meet customer demands.

Sourcing Vehicles

New Vehicles

- **Direct from Manufacturers**: Establish relationships with automotive manufacturers to procure new vehicles directly. Participate in manufacturer incentive programs and promotions to secure competitive pricing and exclusive models.
- **Wholesale Auctions**: Attend dealer-only auctions to purchase new vehicles at wholesale prices. Research market demand and bidding strategies to acquire inventory that aligns with customer preferences.

Used Vehicles

- **Trade-Ins**: Accept trade-in vehicles from customers as part of new vehicle purchases or as standalone transactions. Evaluate trade-ins based on condition, market value, and resale potential.
- **Auctions and Wholesale Markets**: Purchase used vehicles from auctions, wholesale markets, and private sellers. Conduct thorough inspections and vehicle history checks to ensure quality and reliability.
- **Certified Pre-Owned (CPO) Programs**: Partner with manufacturers offering certified pre-owned programs. CPO vehicles undergo rigorous inspections and come with extended warranties, appealing to customers seeking reliability and peace of mind.

Inventory Stocking Strategies

Diversified Inventory Mix

- **Popular Models and Brands**: Stock popular vehicle models and brands that align with customer preferences and market trends. Monitor sales data and customer feedback to adjust inventory mix accordingly.
- **New vs. Used Balance**: Maintain a balanced inventory mix of new and used vehicles to appeal to a diverse customer base. Adjust inventory levels based on seasonal demand, economic trends, and inventory turnover rates.

Pricing and Profit Margins

- **Competitive Pricing**: Set competitive pricing based on market research, competitor analysis, and vehicle condition. Consider factors such as vehicle age, mileage, features, and market demand when pricing inventory.
- **Profit Margins**: Calculate profit margins for each vehicle based on acquisition cost, reconditioning expenses, and anticipated selling price. Strive to achieve profitability while remaining competitive in the marketplace.

Inventory Management Practices

Vehicle Inspection and Reconditioning

- **Thorough Inspections**: Conduct comprehensive inspections for all incoming vehicles to assess mechanical condition, cosmetic appearance, and safety features. Address any necessary repairs or maintenance to enhance vehicle appeal.
- **Detailing and Presentation**: Prioritize vehicle detailing and presentation to create a positive first impression for customers. Clean interiors, polish exteriors, and showcase vehicles in well-lit and organized showroom displays.

Inventory Turnover and Aging

- **Inventory Turnover**: Implement strategies to optimize inventory turnover rates and minimize holding costs. Promote vehicles effectively, offer incentives for quick sales, and monitor aging inventory to prevent depreciation.
- **Seasonal Promotions**: Align inventory management with seasonal promotions and market trends. Offer incentives, discounts, or special financing options to stimulate sales during peak buying seasons or clearance events.

Technology and Tools

Inventory Management Systems

- **Digital Platforms**: Utilize dealership management software (DMS) and customer relationship management (CRM) systems to track inventory levels, monitor vehicle history, and analyze sales performance. Leverage data analytics to make informed inventory decisions.
- **Online Listings**: Maintain an online inventory database with detailed vehicle listings, high-quality photos, and accurate descriptions. Utilize digital marketing channels and automotive marketplaces to reach a broader audience of potential buyers.

Conclusion

Effective inventory management is essential for maintaining profitability, meeting customer expectations, and sustaining growth in your car dealership. By implementing strategic sourcing practices, optimizing inventory stocking strategies, maintaining competitive pricing, and leveraging technology-driven solutions, you can streamline operations and enhance the overall customer experience. In the next chapters, we'll explore sales techniques, customer relationship management, service department operations, and marketing strategies—all aimed at supporting your dealership's success and fostering long-term business growth.

Chapter 8: Sales Techniques and Customer Engagement

Welcome to Chapter 8 of your guide on starting a car dealership! Mastering effective sales techniques and fostering strong customer engagement are key to driving revenue and building a loyal customer base. In this chapter, we'll explore strategies to enhance your sales process, cultivate lasting relationships with customers, and create memorable buying experiences.

Understanding the Sales Process

Customer-Centric Approach

- **Building Rapport**: Establish rapport with customers by greeting them warmly, actively listening to their needs, and demonstrating genuine interest in helping them find the right vehicle.
- **Needs Assessment**: Conduct a thorough needs assessment to understand each customer's preferences, budget constraints, lifestyle requirements, and desired features in a vehicle.
- **Product Knowledge**: Equip your sales team with in-depth knowledge of vehicle features, specifications, safety ratings, and performance capabilities. Demonstrate expertise to instill confidence in customers.

Effective Sales Techniques

Consultative Selling

- **Educate and Advise**: Adopt a consultative selling approach to guide customers through the vehicle selection process. Provide information on available options, financing terms, and incentives tailored to their needs.
- **Demonstration Drives**: Encourage customers to test drive vehicles to experience performance, handling, and comfort firsthand. Highlight unique features and benefits that align with their preferences.

Overcoming Objections

- **Addressing Concerns**: Anticipate and address customer objections regarding pricing, vehicle condition, financing terms, or competitive alternatives. Provide transparent information and options to alleviate concerns.
- **Value Proposition**: Emphasize the value proposition of each vehicle, such as fuel efficiency, safety features, reliability, and resale value. Position your dealership as a trusted advisor offering solutions that meet customer expectations.

Building Customer Relationships

Personalized Customer Service

- **Tailored Recommendations**: Recommend vehicles based on customer preferences, budget, and lifestyle considerations. Offer personalized solutions and follow-up to ensure satisfaction throughout the buying process.
- **Post-Sale Support**: Provide post-sale support, including vehicle delivery, orientation on features, and assistance with registration and paperwork. Follow up with customers to address any questions or concerns.

Loyalty Programs and Incentives

- **Customer Rewards**: Implement loyalty programs, referral incentives, and exclusive offers for repeat customers. Recognize loyal patrons with special discounts, service perks, or VIP events to foster long-term relationships.

Enhancing Customer Experience

Streamlined Processes

- **Efficient Transactions**: Streamline paperwork and financing processes to minimize wait times and enhance customer

convenience. Utilize digital tools and e-signature capabilities for efficient document management.
- **Transparent Communication**: Maintain open communication channels with customers regarding pricing, financing options, vehicle availability, and service scheduling. Build trust through honesty and transparency.

Feedback and Continuous Improvement

- **Customer Feedback**: Solicit feedback from customers to gauge satisfaction levels and identify areas for improvement. Use feedback to refine sales techniques, enhance service offerings, and adapt to changing market preferences.

Leveraging Technology

Digital Engagement

- **Online Presence**: Maintain a user-friendly website with detailed vehicle listings, virtual showroom tours, and online appointment scheduling. Utilize social media platforms and digital marketing campaigns to engage prospective customers.
- **CRM Systems**: Utilize customer relationship management (CRM) software to track customer interactions, manage leads, and personalize follow-up communications. Leverage data analytics to predict customer behavior and preferences.

Conclusion

Mastering effective sales techniques and fostering strong customer engagement are critical for the success of your car dealership. By adopting a customer-centric approach, enhancing sales skills, building lasting relationships, and leveraging technology-driven solutions, you can create memorable buying experiences that differentiate your dealership in a competitive market. In the next chapters, we'll explore service department operations, marketing strategies, community engagement, and staff development—all essential components for achieving sustained growth and profitability in the automotive retail industry.

Chapter 9: Service Department Operations and Customer Satisfaction

Welcome to Chapter 9 of your comprehensive guide on starting a car dealership! A well-managed service department plays a crucial role in enhancing customer satisfaction, building loyalty, and generating recurring revenue for your dealership. This chapter will explore best practices for service department operations, maintaining high standards of customer service, and maximizing efficiency.

Importance of a Service Department

Customer Retention and Loyalty

- **Retention Strategy**: A reliable service department fosters customer loyalty by providing quality maintenance, repairs, and personalized service experiences. Satisfied customers are more likely to return for future vehicle servicing and recommend your dealership to others.

Revenue Generation

- **Profit Center**: The service department contributes significantly to dealership revenue through service fees, parts sales, and potential upsells such as extended warranties, accessories, and maintenance packages.

Setting Up Your Service Department

Facility and Equipment

- **Workshop Layout**: Design a functional layout that optimizes workflow efficiency and technician productivity. Allocate space for service bays, diagnostic equipment, tools, and parts storage.
- **Diagnostic Tools**: Invest in state-of-the-art diagnostic tools and equipment to accurately diagnose vehicle issues and perform repairs efficiently. Ensure technicians receive training on equipment operation and maintenance.

Service Staffing

- **Qualified Technicians**: Recruit skilled and certified technicians with expertise in various vehicle makes and models. Provide ongoing training to keep technicians updated on industry advancements, new technologies, and manufacturer-specific service protocols.
- **Service Advisors**: Hire knowledgeable service advisors to assist customers, schedule appointments, explain service recommendations, and ensure clear communication throughout the service process.

Delivering Exceptional Customer Service

Service Consultation

- **Personalized Approach**: Conduct thorough consultations with customers to understand their vehicle concerns, maintenance history, and service expectations. Address any questions or concerns to build trust and transparency.
- **Educational Approach**: Educate customers on recommended maintenance services, warranty coverage, and the importance of regular vehicle inspections to prolong vehicle lifespan and prevent costly repairs.

Transparent Communication

- **Service Updates**: Provide timely updates to customers regarding service progress, estimated completion times, and any additional repairs or parts needed. Maintain open communication channels via phone, email, or text messaging.
- **Cost Estimates**: Offer detailed cost estimates upfront and obtain customer approval before proceeding with repairs or maintenance beyond the initial service request. Explain pricing breakdowns and justify recommended services.

Service Department Best Practices

Quality Assurance

- **Thorough Inspections**: Conduct comprehensive vehicle inspections before and after service to ensure quality workmanship and customer satisfaction. Use inspection checklists to document findings and recommendations.
- **Guarantees and Warranties**: Offer warranties on parts and labor to reassure customers of service quality and provide peace of mind. Honor manufacturer warranties and address any issues promptly to uphold customer trust.

Appointment Scheduling

- **Efficient Scheduling**: Implement an online appointment scheduling system or mobile app for customers to book service appointments conveniently. Manage service bay utilization to minimize wait times and maximize technician efficiency.

Technology Integration

Service Management Software

- **DMS Integration**: Integrate service management software with your dealership management system (DMS) to streamline scheduling, track service history, manage parts inventory, and generate service reports.
- **Customer Portal**: Offer a customer portal where clients can view service history, schedule appointments, approve repair orders, and receive service reminders. Enhance convenience and accessibility for tech-savvy customers.

Conclusion

A well-run service department is essential for enhancing customer satisfaction, generating revenue, and maintaining long-term profitability for your car dealership. By investing in facility design, state-of-the-art equipment, qualified personnel, and customer-centric service practices, you can differentiate your dealership and build a reputation for excellence in automotive service. In the next chapters, we'll explore marketing strategies, community engagement initiatives, staff training and development, and operational excellence—all aimed at supporting your dealership's growth and success in the competitive automotive retail industry.

Chapter 10: Marketing Strategies for Your Car Dealership

Welcome to Chapter 10 of your guide on starting a car dealership! Effective marketing is essential for attracting customers, building brand awareness, and driving sales. In this chapter, we'll explore proven marketing strategies and tactics to promote your dealership, connect with your target audience, and achieve sustainable growth.

Developing Your Marketing Plan

Target Audience Identification

- **Customer Segmentation**: Identify and segment your target audience based on demographics (age, gender, income), psychographics (lifestyle, preferences), and geographic location. Tailor marketing efforts to resonate with each segment's unique needs and preferences.

Competitive Analysis

- **Competitor Research**: Analyze competitors' marketing strategies, target audience engagement tactics, pricing models, and promotional offers. Identify gaps and opportunities to differentiate your dealership in the marketplace.

Digital Marketing Strategies

Website Optimization

- **User-Friendly Design**: Ensure your dealership website is user-friendly, visually appealing, and mobile-responsive. Provide intuitive navigation, fast loading times, and clear calls-to-action (CTAs) to encourage visitor engagement.
- **Search Engine Optimization (SEO)**: Optimize website content with relevant keywords, meta descriptions, and alt tags to improve search engine rankings. Create valuable, informative

content such as blogs, vehicle reviews, and buying guides to attract organic traffic.

Pay-Per-Click Advertising (PPC)

- **Targeted Campaigns**: Launch PPC campaigns on search engines (Google Ads) and social media platforms (Facebook Ads) to target potential customers based on search queries, demographics, and interests. Monitor campaign performance and adjust bids to maximize ROI.

Social Media Marketing

- **Engagement and Brand Building**: Maintain an active presence on social media platforms (Facebook, Instagram, Twitter) to engage with customers, showcase inventory, share dealership updates, and respond to inquiries in real-time. Use visually appealing content such as photos, videos, and customer testimonials to build brand credibility.

Content Marketing

Blogging and Content Creation

- **Educational Content**: Publish informative blogs, articles, and videos that address common customer questions, automotive trends, maintenance tips, and vehicle reviews. Establish your dealership as a trusted authority in the automotive industry.

Email Marketing

- **Customer Relationship Building**: Develop personalized email campaigns to nurture leads, promote special offers, announce new inventory arrivals, and encourage repeat business. Segment email lists based on customer preferences and buying history for targeted messaging.

Traditional Marketing Tactics

Direct Mail Campaigns

- **Targeted Mailers**: Send targeted direct mail campaigns to local residents, previous customers, and prospects based on demographics and purchase behavior. Include promotional offers, event invitations, and dealership updates to drive foot traffic and sales.

Event Marketing

- **Community Events**: Host or sponsor community events, car shows, or charity drives to increase brand visibility, foster goodwill, and attract potential customers. Distribute promotional materials and engage attendees with interactive activities or test drives.

Customer Referral Programs

Incentivizing Referrals

- **Referral Rewards**: Implement a referral program offering incentives such as cash rewards, service discounts, or gift cards to customers who refer friends, family, or colleagues to your dealership. Encourage satisfied customers to become brand advocates.

Measuring Success

Performance Metrics

- **Key Performance Indicators (KPIs)**: Track metrics such as website traffic, lead conversion rates, click-through rates (CTR) on ads, social media engagement, and customer retention rates. Use analytics tools to evaluate campaign effectiveness and make data-driven marketing decisions.

Conclusion

Implementing effective marketing strategies is essential for driving traffic to your dealership, increasing sales, and fostering long-term customer relationships. By developing a comprehensive marketing plan, leveraging digital and traditional marketing channels, creating engaging content, and measuring campaign performance, you can position your car dealership for success in a competitive market. In the next chapters, we'll explore customer service excellence, staff training, operational efficiency, and community engagement—all vital components for building a thriving automotive retail business.

Chapter 11: Customer Service Excellence

Welcome to Chapter 11 of your journey towards running a successful car dealership! In this chapter, we'll delve into the importance of delivering exceptional customer service, strategies for creating memorable experiences, and fostering long-lasting relationships with your valued customers.

The Importance of Customer Service

Building Trust and Loyalty

Customer service is not just about resolving issues; it's about creating positive interactions that build trust and loyalty. When customers feel valued and respected, they are more likely to return to your dealership for future purchases and recommend your services to others.

Differentiation in a Competitive Market

In a competitive automotive industry, excellent customer service can set your dealership apart from competitors. It's often the deciding factor for customers choosing where to buy their vehicles and where to bring them for maintenance and repairs.

Strategies for Delivering Exceptional Customer Service

Training and Empowerment

- **Employee Training**: Invest in comprehensive training programs for dealership staff, emphasizing communication skills, product knowledge, and conflict resolution. Ensure employees understand the importance of customer satisfaction in every interaction.
- **Empowerment**: Empower frontline staff to make decisions and resolve issues promptly without needing to escalate concerns. Provide guidelines and support to enable employees to handle customer inquiries and complaints effectively.

Personalized Interactions

- **Know Your Customers**: Take the time to learn about your customers' preferences, past purchases, and service history. Use customer relationship management (CRM) systems to track interactions and personalize service experiences.
- **Tailored Recommendations**: Offer personalized recommendations based on customer needs and preferences. Whether it's suggesting a vehicle upgrade or recommending maintenance services, show customers that you understand their unique requirements.

Creating Memorable Customer Experiences

Positive First Impressions

- **Warm Welcome**: Greet customers with a friendly smile and genuine enthusiasm upon their arrival at the dealership. Offer refreshments and ensure they feel comfortable while browsing vehicles or waiting for service.
- **Clean and Inviting Environment**: Maintain a clean and organized showroom, service area, and customer waiting area. A well-presented environment reflects professionalism and attention to detail.

Communication Excellence

- **Clear Communication**: Communicate clearly and transparently with customers throughout the buying process, service appointments, and follow-up interactions. Provide updates on vehicle status, estimated completion times, and any additional service recommendations.
- **Active Listening**: Practice active listening to understand customer concerns and preferences. Repeat back information to ensure mutual understanding and address any misunderstandings promptly.

Resolving Customer Issues

Prompt Resolution

- **Proactive Approach**: Anticipate potential issues and address them proactively to prevent customer dissatisfaction. Empower staff to handle complaints promptly and escalate unresolved issues to management when necessary.
- **Follow-Up**: Follow up with customers after service appointments or vehicle purchases to ensure satisfaction. Address any lingering concerns and demonstrate your commitment to resolving issues effectively.

Feedback and Continuous Improvement

Soliciting Feedback

- **Customer Surveys**: Conduct customer satisfaction surveys to gather feedback on dealership experiences, service quality, and areas for improvement. Use survey results to identify trends, address concerns, and implement changes to enhance service delivery.
- **Online Reviews**: Monitor online reviews and social media comments to gauge customer sentiment and respond promptly to feedback—both positive and negative. Show appreciation for positive reviews and take constructive criticism as an opportunity for growth.

Conclusion

Delivering exceptional customer service is fundamental to building a successful and reputable car dealership. By prioritizing customer satisfaction, investing in staff training, personalizing interactions, resolving issues promptly, and soliciting feedback for continuous improvement, you can create memorable experiences that inspire customer loyalty and drive business growth. In the next chapters, we'll explore operational efficiency, staff development, community engagement, and innovative strategies to further enhance your dealership's success in the competitive automotive market.

Chapter 12: Staff Development and Team Building

Welcome to Chapter 12 of your comprehensive guide on starting and managing a successful car dealership! In this chapter, we'll explore the importance of staff development, effective team building strategies, and fostering a positive work environment to maximize productivity and employee satisfaction.

Importance of Staff Development

Enhancing Skills and Knowledge

Investing in staff development not only enhances the skills and knowledge of your employees but also improves overall dealership performance. Well-trained staff are better equipped to handle customer inquiries, resolve issues efficiently, and contribute to the dealership's success.

Employee Engagement and Retention

Offering opportunities for growth and career advancement increases employee engagement and reduces turnover rates. Engaged employees are more likely to stay committed to their roles, deliver exceptional customer service, and contribute positively to the dealership's culture.

Strategies for Staff Development

Training Programs

- **Onboarding**: Implement a structured onboarding program for new hires to familiarize them with dealership policies, procedures, and job responsibilities. Provide training on customer service standards, product knowledge, and sales techniques.
- **Continued Education**: Offer ongoing training sessions, workshops, and certifications to keep employees updated on industry trends, new vehicle models, technological

advancements, and best practices in automotive sales and service.

Cross-Training Opportunities

- **Skill Diversification**: Cross-train employees across different departments, such as sales, service, finance, and administrative roles. This not only broadens their skill set but also promotes teamwork and collaboration within the dealership.

Mentorship Programs

- **Experienced Mentors**: Pair new employees with experienced mentors who can provide guidance, share expertise, and offer support as they acclimate to their roles. Mentorship programs foster professional growth and create a supportive learning environment.

Fostering a Positive Work Environment

Leadership and Communication

- **Transparent Communication**: Maintain open lines of communication between management and staff. Encourage feedback, address concerns promptly, and recognize employee contributions to foster a culture of trust and mutual respect.
- **Leadership Development**: Provide leadership training and opportunities for employees interested in advancing to supervisory or management roles. Develop future leaders within your dealership who can inspire teams and drive organizational success.

Team Building Activities

- **Collaborative Events**: Organize team-building activities, such as retreats, workshops, and social gatherings, to strengthen bonds among employees. Foster camaraderie, improve communication skills, and celebrate team achievements.

Recognizing and Rewarding Excellence

Employee Recognition Programs

- **Achievement Awards**: Establish recognition programs to acknowledge employee accomplishments, outstanding performance, and milestones. Reward achievements with incentives such as bonuses, gift cards, or public recognition during team meetings.
- **Incentive Programs**: Implement sales incentives and performance-based bonuses to motivate employees and drive productivity. Align incentives with dealership goals and encourage healthy competition among team members.

Supporting Work-Life Balance

Flexible Policies

- **Work-Life Balance**: Offer flexible scheduling options, remote work opportunities (if feasible), and paid time off to support employees' personal well-being and family commitments. Balance work demands with a supportive, accommodating workplace culture.

Conclusion

Investing in staff development and fostering a positive work environment are essential for creating a motivated and high-performing team at your car dealership. By providing comprehensive training, promoting career growth opportunities, encouraging teamwork, recognizing achievements, and supporting work-life balance, you can attract top talent, retain skilled employees, and cultivate a culture of excellence. In the next chapters, we'll explore operational efficiency, customer engagement strategies, community involvement, and innovative approaches to further strengthen your dealership's position in the competitive automotive market.

Chapter 13: Operational Efficiency and Process Optimization

Welcome to Chapter 13 of your guide on managing a successful car dealership! In this chapter, we'll delve into the importance of operational efficiency, strategies for optimizing dealership processes, and achieving maximum productivity while delivering exceptional customer service.

Importance of Operational Efficiency

Enhancing Customer Experience

Operational efficiency plays a crucial role in enhancing the overall customer experience at your dealership. Streamlined processes reduce wait times, improve service delivery, and ensure a seamless buying and service experience for customers.

Cost Management and Profitability

Efficient operations help minimize overhead costs, maximize resource utilization, and enhance profitability. By optimizing processes and reducing waste, you can allocate resources more effectively and maintain competitive pricing.

Strategies for Process Optimization

Workflow Analysis

- **Process Mapping**: Conduct a thorough analysis of dealership workflows, from vehicle acquisition and sales to service appointments and administrative tasks. Identify bottlenecks, inefficiencies, and areas for improvement.
- **Standard Operating Procedures (SOPs)**: Develop and implement standardized procedures for routine tasks and operations. SOPs ensure consistency, clarity in roles, and adherence to best practices across departments.

Technology Integration

- **Dealership Management System (DMS)**: Utilize a robust DMS to automate inventory management, sales tracking, customer data management, and financial transactions. Integrate DMS with CRM systems for seamless information flow and enhanced customer service.
- **Digital Tools**: Adopt digital tools and software for appointment scheduling, document management, online payments, and customer communications. Leverage technology to streamline processes, reduce paperwork, and improve operational transparency.

Inventory Management and Turnover

Efficient Inventory Practices

- **Inventory Turnover**: Implement strategies to optimize inventory turnover rates and minimize holding costs. Monitor vehicle demand trends, adjust stocking levels accordingly, and prioritize sales incentives to move inventory efficiently.
- **Vehicle Reconditioning**: Streamline vehicle reconditioning processes to minimize turnaround times between acquisitions and sales. Ensure vehicles are thoroughly inspected, reconditioned to high standards, and ready for showroom presentation.

Employee Efficiency and Training

Staff Productivity

- **Training and Development**: Continuously invest in employee training to enhance skills, product knowledge, and customer service capabilities. Equip staff with tools and resources to perform their roles efficiently and contribute to overall operational success.

- **Performance Metrics**: Establish key performance indicators (KPIs) for each department and role to measure productivity, service quality, and customer satisfaction. Provide regular feedback and performance reviews to encourage continuous improvement.

Customer Relationship Management (CRM)

Effective CRM Practices

- **Data Management**: Maintain accurate customer records, purchase history, and service preferences within the CRM system. Use customer data to personalize interactions, anticipate needs, and foster long-term relationships.
- **Follow-Up and Feedback**: Implement automated follow-up processes for sales inquiries, service appointments, and customer feedback. Solicit customer reviews, address concerns promptly, and use feedback to refine service offerings.

Continuous Improvement Culture

Kaizen Philosophy

- **Kaizen Principles**: Embrace a culture of continuous improvement where employees are encouraged to suggest process enhancements, innovation, and efficiency gains. Foster a collaborative environment where ideas are valued and implemented.

Feedback Loops

- **Feedback Mechanisms**: Establish mechanisms for gathering employee feedback on operational challenges, workflow bottlenecks, and improvement opportunities. Encourage open communication and empower staff to contribute to operational excellence.

Conclusion

Operational efficiency is essential for achieving sustainable growth, maximizing profitability, and delivering exceptional customer experiences at your car dealership. By optimizing workflows, integrating technology, managing inventory effectively, investing in employee training, leveraging CRM systems, and fostering a culture of continuous improvement, you can streamline operations and position your dealership for long-term success in the competitive automotive market. In the next chapters, we'll explore community engagement strategies, marketing innovations, financial management, and leadership practices—all aimed at further strengthening your dealership's position and reputation in the industry.

Chapter 14: Financial Management for Your Car Dealership

Welcome to Chapter 14 of your comprehensive guide on managing a successful car dealership! In this chapter, we'll explore the fundamentals of financial management tailored specifically to the automotive retail industry. Understanding and effectively managing finances is crucial for sustaining profitability, minimizing risks, and achieving long-term financial stability.

Importance of Financial Management

Strategic Decision-Making

Financial management provides valuable insights and data-driven decision-making tools that guide strategic planning and operational efficiency. By monitoring financial health, analyzing performance metrics, and forecasting trends, you can make informed decisions to optimize profitability and mitigate financial risks.

Compliance and Accountability

Adhering to financial regulations, tax obligations, and industry standards ensures legal compliance and enhances transparency. Maintaining accurate financial records and conducting regular audits demonstrate accountability to stakeholders, investors, and regulatory authorities.

Key Financial Concepts

Budgeting and Forecasting

- **Budget Development**: Develop a comprehensive budget that outlines projected revenues, expenses, and profit margins for each operational area, including sales, service, parts, and administrative functions. Monitor actual performance against budgeted targets and adjust forecasts as needed.

- **Financial Forecasting**: Use historical data, market trends, and economic indicators to forecast future sales volumes, cash flow projections, and capital requirements. Anticipate seasonal fluctuations, industry cycles, and external factors that may impact financial performance.

Cash Flow Management

- **Cash Flow Analysis**: Monitor cash inflows and outflows to maintain liquidity and meet financial obligations, such as payroll, inventory purchases, and operational expenses. Implement strategies to accelerate receivables, optimize inventory turnover, and manage supplier payments.
- **Working Capital Management**: Manage working capital effectively to support day-to-day operations and business growth initiatives. Balance inventory levels, receivables collection, and payables management to optimize cash flow and minimize financing costs.

Financial Reporting and Analysis

Performance Metrics

- **Key Performance Indicators (KPIs)**: Track financial metrics, such as gross profit margins, inventory turnover ratios, sales per employee, and return on investment (ROI). Use financial ratios and benchmarks to evaluate profitability, efficiency, and overall financial health.
- **Financial Statements**: Prepare accurate and timely financial statements, including income statements, balance sheets, and cash flow statements. Analyze variances, trends, and deviations from financial goals to identify areas for improvement and strategic adjustments.

Cost Control and Expense Management

Operational Efficiency

- **Cost Reduction Strategies**: Identify opportunities to reduce operating expenses, such as overhead costs, utilities, and non-essential expenditures. Negotiate favorable terms with suppliers, optimize logistics and inventory management, and implement energy-saving initiatives.
- **Expense Monitoring**: Establish expense controls and approval processes to monitor discretionary spending and ensure alignment with budgetary guidelines. Conduct regular reviews of expense reports and implement corrective actions as needed.

Financing and Capital Investment

Capital Expenditure Planning

- **Investment Decisions**: Evaluate capital investment opportunities, such as facility upgrades, equipment purchases, and technology enhancements, based on return on investment (ROI) and strategic priorities. Secure financing options with favorable terms and consider tax implications.
- **Debt Management**: Manage debt obligations responsibly by monitoring debt levels, interest rates, and repayment schedules. Evaluate refinancing opportunities to lower interest costs and improve cash flow management.

Risk Management and Contingency Planning

Risk Assessment

- **Risk Identification**: Conduct risk assessments to identify potential threats to financial stability, including market volatility, economic downturns, regulatory changes, and operational risks. Develop contingency plans and mitigation strategies to minimize impact on business operations.
- **Insurance Coverage**: Maintain adequate insurance coverage, such as property insurance, liability insurance, and business interruption insurance, to protect against unforeseen events and mitigate financial losses.

Conclusion

Effective financial management is essential for driving profitability, sustaining growth, and ensuring long-term success in the competitive automotive retail industry. By implementing sound budgeting practices, optimizing cash flow management, analyzing financial performance, controlling costs, making strategic investments, and mitigating risks, you can strengthen your dealership's financial position and achieve your business objectives. In the next chapters, we'll explore leadership strategies, community engagement initiatives, marketing innovations, and customer service excellence—all integral components for building a resilient and thriving car dealership business.

Chapter 15: Community Engagement and Building Relationships

Welcome to Chapter 15 of your comprehensive guide on running a successful car dealership! In this chapter, we'll explore the importance of community engagement, strategies for building meaningful relationships with local communities, and how these efforts can contribute to your dealership's success.

Importance of Community Engagement

Building Trust and Credibility

Community engagement fosters trust and credibility with local residents, businesses, and organizations. By actively participating in community events, supporting local initiatives, and demonstrating a commitment to community well-being, your dealership becomes a trusted member of the neighborhood.

Brand Awareness and Reputation

Engaging with the community increases brand visibility and enhances your dealership's reputation. Positive interactions, sponsorships, and community involvement initiatives create a favorable impression among potential customers, leading to increased foot traffic and sales opportunities.

Strategies for Community Engagement

Sponsorship and Partnerships

- **Local Events**: Sponsor or participate in community events, such as festivals, charity drives, youth sports teams, and school fundraisers. Display banners, distribute promotional materials, and offer vehicle displays or test drives to engage attendees.
- **Partnerships**: Collaborate with local businesses, non-profit organizations, and community groups on mutually beneficial initiatives. Develop sponsorship packages or donation programs

that align with your dealership's values and community priorities.

Educational Workshops and Seminars

- **Consumer Education**: Host workshops, seminars, or webinars on automotive topics, such as car maintenance tips, safe driving practices, and vehicle technology demonstrations. Provide valuable information to community members and establish your dealership as a trusted resource.

Customer Appreciation Events

- **Exclusive Events**: Organize customer appreciation events, VIP nights, or owner clinics for current and prospective customers. Offer discounts on services, refreshments, entertainment, and personalized consultations to enhance customer loyalty and satisfaction.

Supporting Local Causes

Philanthropic Initiatives

- **Charitable Contributions**: Donate to local charities, community organizations, or youth programs that align with your dealership's values and mission. Sponsor charitable events, volunteer as a team, or organize donation drives to make a positive impact in the community.

Environmental Stewardship

- **Green Initiatives**: Implement environmentally friendly practices, such as recycling programs, energy-efficient upgrades, and promoting eco-friendly vehicle options. Demonstrate your dealership's commitment to sustainability and corporate social responsibility.

Digital and Social Media Engagement

Online Community Building

- **Social Media Presence**: Maintain active social media profiles (Facebook, Instagram, Twitter) to share community involvement efforts, dealership news, and customer testimonials. Engage with followers, respond to comments, and promote community events digitally.
- **Local Content**: Create content that resonates with local audiences, such as highlighting community events, featuring customer stories, and showcasing dealership contributions to the community. Encourage user-generated content and community participation online.

Measuring Impact and Feedback

Evaluation Metrics

- **Community Impact**: Measure the success of community engagement efforts through metrics such as event attendance, media coverage, social media engagement, and customer feedback. Evaluate return on investment (ROI) in terms of brand awareness and customer acquisition.
- **Feedback Collection**: Solicit feedback from community members, event attendees, and customers through surveys, online reviews, and direct interactions. Use insights to refine engagement strategies, improve event planning, and strengthen community relationships.

Conclusion

Community engagement is more than just a marketing strategy—it's about building genuine connections, supporting local causes, and contributing positively to the communities you serve. By investing in meaningful relationships, sponsoring local events, educating consumers, and demonstrating corporate citizenship, your dealership can establish a strong presence, enhance brand reputation, and foster customer loyalty. In the next chapters, we'll explore leadership principles, marketing innovations, operational excellence, and customer service strategies—all integral components for achieving sustainable growth and success in the competitive automotive retail industry.

Chapter 16: Innovation in Automotive Retail

Welcome to Chapter 16 of your comprehensive guide on automotive retail management! In this chapter, we'll explore the exciting realm of innovation within the automotive industry, focusing on emerging trends, technological advancements, and innovative strategies that can propel your dealership forward.

Embracing Technological Advancements

Digital Transformation

The automotive industry is undergoing a digital revolution, with advancements in technology reshaping every aspect of the dealership experience. Embracing these innovations can enhance operational efficiency, improve customer engagement, and drive competitive advantage.

Customer-Centric Technologies

- **Online Sales Platforms**: Develop intuitive and user-friendly online sales platforms that allow customers to browse inventory, schedule test drives, and complete purchases from the comfort of their homes. Incorporate virtual reality (VR) or augmented reality (AR) for immersive vehicle experiences.
- **Digital Showrooms**: Implement digital showrooms equipped with interactive displays, touchscreen kiosks, and multimedia presentations to showcase vehicle features, customization options, and pricing information in a dynamic and engaging manner.

Enhancing Customer Experience

Personalization and Customization

- **Data-Driven Insights**: Utilize customer relationship management (CRM) systems and data analytics to gather

insights into customer preferences, purchase behavior, and service history. Personalize interactions, tailor marketing offers, and anticipate customer needs.
- **Vehicle Customization**: Offer personalized vehicle customization options, such as color choices, accessories, and interior features, to cater to individual tastes and preferences. Use digital tools to visualize modifications and enhance the buying experience.

Leveraging Artificial Intelligence (AI) and Machine Learning

AI-Powered Solutions

- **Chatbots and Virtual Assistants**: Implement AI-powered chatbots on your website and social media channels to provide instant customer support, answer inquiries, schedule appointments, and guide users through the buying process. Enhance customer service efficiency and responsiveness.
- **Predictive Analytics**: Utilize machine learning algorithms to analyze customer data, predict buying patterns, and optimize inventory management. Anticipate demand trends, identify sales opportunities, and streamline supply chain operations.

Sustainable and Eco-Friendly Initiatives

Green Technologies

- **Electric and Hybrid Vehicles**: Showcase eco-friendly vehicle options, such as electric and hybrid models, and promote their environmental benefits. Offer incentives, educational resources, and charging infrastructure to support adoption among environmentally conscious consumers.
- **Sustainable Practices**: Implement sustainable business practices, such as energy-efficient operations, recycling programs, and paperless initiatives, to minimize environmental impact and enhance corporate social responsibility (CSR) credentials.

Integration of Internet of Things (IoT) and Connectivity

Connected Vehicles

- **IoT Integration**: Equip vehicles with IoT sensors and connectivity features that enable remote diagnostics, predictive maintenance alerts, and real-time vehicle tracking. Enhance vehicle safety, performance monitoring, and personalized customer service offerings.
- **Smart Dealership Solutions**: Deploy IoT-enabled systems within the dealership, such as smart inventory management, automated service scheduling, and digital signage. Improve operational efficiency, reduce costs, and enhance customer experience.

Continuous Learning and Adaptation

Innovation Culture

- **Adaptive Strategies**: Foster an innovation culture within your dealership that encourages experimentation, embraces change, and values creativity. Empower employees to propose innovative ideas, pilot new technologies, and collaborate on process improvements.
- **Industry Collaboration**: Stay abreast of industry trends, participate in automotive conferences, and engage with technology partners and industry experts to explore emerging technologies and best practices. Collaborate with manufacturers and suppliers to pilot new products and services.

Conclusion

Innovation is essential for staying competitive and meeting evolving customer expectations in the automotive retail sector. By leveraging technological advancements, enhancing customer experiences through personalization and AI-driven solutions, promoting sustainable initiatives, integrating IoT connectivity, and fostering an innovation-driven culture, your dealership can differentiate itself in the marketplace and achieve sustainable growth. In the next chapters, we'll explore leadership strategies, operational excellence, financial management, and customer service innovations—all crucial components for building a resilient and successful automotive retail business.

Chapter 17: Marketing Strategies for Automotive Dealerships

Welcome to Chapter 17 of your guide on managing a successful car dealership! In this chapter, we'll explore effective marketing strategies tailored specifically to the automotive industry. From digital marketing tactics to traditional advertising methods, we'll cover how to attract, engage, and retain customers in today's competitive marketplace.

Understanding Automotive Consumer Behavior

Customer Journey Mapping

Understanding the automotive consumer journey is essential for crafting targeted marketing strategies. From initial research to vehicle purchase and post-sale service, each stage presents opportunities to influence consumer decisions through effective marketing tactics.

Market Segmentation

- **Demographic Analysis**: Identify key demographic segments, such as age, income level, lifestyle preferences, and vehicle preferences. Tailor marketing messages and campaigns to resonate with specific customer segments and address their unique needs.
- **Behavioral Insights**: Analyze consumer behaviors, purchase motivations, and decision-making processes. Use data analytics and customer feedback to refine marketing strategies and deliver personalized experiences that drive engagement and conversions.

Digital Marketing Strategies

Online Presence and Visibility

- **Search Engine Optimization (SEO)**: Optimize your dealership's website with relevant keywords, localized content, and mobile-friendly design to improve search engine rankings. Ensure easy

navigation, fast loading times, and compelling calls-to-action (CTAs) to attract organic traffic.
- **Pay-Per-Click (PPC) Advertising**: Launch targeted PPC campaigns on search engines (e.g., Google Ads) and social media platforms (e.g., Facebook, Instagram) to drive qualified traffic to your website. Use geo-targeting and retargeting strategies to reach local audiences and capture leads.

Content Marketing

- **Educational Content**: Create informative and engaging content, such as blog posts, videos, and infographics, that address common automotive questions, maintenance tips, vehicle reviews, and industry trends. Establish your dealership as a trusted resource and build credibility with potential customers.
- **Customer Testimonials**: Showcase customer testimonials, reviews, and success stories on your website and social media channels. Encourage satisfied customers to share their experiences and recommendations, which can influence purchase decisions and build trust.

Social Media Engagement

Building Relationships

- **Social Media Platforms**: Maintain active profiles on popular social media platforms to connect with current and prospective customers. Share dealership updates, promotions, vehicle features, and community involvement initiatives. Engage with followers through comments, messages, and live interactions.
- **User-Generated Content**: Encourage customers to share photos and videos of their vehicle purchases or service experiences on social media. Repost user-generated content to amplify brand advocacy, foster community engagement, and attract new audiences.

Customer Relationship Management (CRM)

Email Marketing Campaigns

- **Personalized Campaigns**: Segment your email list based on customer preferences, purchase history, and service records. Send personalized email campaigns with relevant offers, maintenance reminders, and exclusive promotions to nurture customer relationships and encourage repeat business.
- **Automated Follow-Ups**: Set up automated email sequences to follow up with leads, schedule service reminders, and send thank-you notes after vehicle purchases. Use CRM software to track email engagement metrics and optimize campaign performance.

Traditional Marketing Tactics

Local Advertising

- **Radio and TV Commercials**: Create compelling radio and TV commercials that highlight dealership promotions, new vehicle arrivals, and special events. Use local media outlets to reach a broad audience and reinforce brand awareness within your community.
- **Direct Mail Campaigns**: Design targeted direct mail campaigns, such as postcards, flyers, and newsletters, to reach local households and businesses. Include promotional offers, dealership updates, and personalized messages to drive traffic to your showroom.

Measuring Marketing Effectiveness

Performance Analytics

- **Key Performance Indicators (KPIs)**: Monitor marketing KPIs, such as website traffic, conversion rates, lead generation, cost per acquisition (CPA), and return on investment (ROI). Use analytics tools to track campaign performance, identify trends, and optimize marketing spend.

- **Customer Feedback**: Gather customer feedback through surveys, online reviews, and social media interactions. Use insights to evaluate customer satisfaction, refine marketing strategies, and address areas for improvement in service delivery and customer experience.

Conclusion

Effective marketing is crucial for attracting, engaging, and retaining customers in the competitive automotive retail industry. By leveraging digital marketing strategies, nurturing customer relationships through CRM initiatives, utilizing traditional advertising tactics, and measuring marketing effectiveness with performance analytics, your dealership can strengthen its market position, drive sales growth, and build a loyal customer base. In the next chapters, we'll explore leadership principles, operational excellence, financial management, and customer service innovations—all essential components for achieving long-term success in automotive retail.

Chapter 18: Customer Service Excellence

Welcome to Chapter 18 of your comprehensive guide on managing a successful car dealership! In this chapter, we'll delve into the principles and practices of delivering exceptional customer service. Providing a remarkable customer experience is crucial for building loyalty, enhancing reputation, and driving repeat business.

Importance of Customer Service

Building Trust and Loyalty

Exceptional customer service builds trust and loyalty among your clients. Customers who feel valued and well-treated are more likely to return for future purchases, recommend your dealership to others, and leave positive reviews.

Competitive Advantage

In a competitive market, outstanding customer service can set your dealership apart. While products and prices may be similar across dealerships, the quality of customer service can be a significant differentiator.

Customer Service Best Practices

Personalized Attention

- **Know Your Customers**: Take the time to understand your customers' needs, preferences, and pain points. Use CRM systems to track their history with your dealership and personalize interactions based on their past experiences and preferences.
- **Listen Actively**: Active listening involves fully concentrating on what the customer is saying, understanding their message, responding thoughtfully, and remembering details for future

interactions. This shows customers that you genuinely care about their needs.

Transparent Communication

- **Honesty and Integrity**: Always provide honest information about products, services, pricing, and financing options. Avoid overselling or making unrealistic promises. Transparency builds trust and credibility.
- **Clear and Timely Updates**: Keep customers informed about the status of their vehicle purchase, service appointments, or any issues they may be facing. Timely updates via phone, email, or text can prevent misunderstandings and show that you respect their time.

Creating a Welcoming Environment

Physical Space

- **Clean and Comfortable Facilities**: Ensure that your dealership's showroom, waiting areas, and service departments are clean, comfortable, and inviting. Offer amenities such as refreshments, Wi-Fi, and entertainment to enhance the customer experience.
- **Friendly Atmosphere**: Foster a friendly and professional atmosphere where customers feel welcome. Train staff to greet customers warmly and assist them promptly upon arrival.

Training and Empowering Staff

Customer Service Training

- **Ongoing Training Programs**: Implement comprehensive training programs for all employees, focusing on customer service skills, product knowledge, and effective communication techniques. Regularly update training materials to reflect new products, services, and customer service standards.

- **Role-Playing Scenarios**: Use role-playing exercises to help staff practice handling various customer interactions, including difficult situations. This prepares them to respond confidently and effectively in real-world scenarios.

Empowerment and Autonomy

- **Empower Decision-Making**: Give employees the authority to make decisions that benefit the customer, such as offering discounts, resolving complaints, or providing special accommodations. Empowered employees can address issues swiftly and enhance customer satisfaction.

Handling Complaints and Feedback

Effective Complaint Resolution

- **Listen and Empathize**: When a customer has a complaint, listen to their concerns without interrupting and show empathy for their situation. Acknowledge their feelings and reassure them that their issue will be addressed.
- **Swift Resolution**: Resolve complaints as quickly as possible. Keep the customer informed about the steps being taken and follow up to ensure their satisfaction with the resolution.

Encouraging Feedback

- **Solicit Feedback**: Actively seek feedback from customers through surveys, online reviews, and direct conversations. Use this feedback to identify areas for improvement and implement changes that enhance the customer experience.
- **Show Appreciation**: Thank customers for their feedback, whether positive or negative. This shows that you value their input and are committed to continuous improvement.

Going the Extra Mile

Exceeding Expectations

- **Surprise and Delight**: Look for opportunities to exceed customer expectations with small gestures, such as a thank-you note, a follow-up call, or a complimentary car wash. These thoughtful actions can leave a lasting positive impression.
- **Customer Loyalty Programs**: Implement loyalty programs that reward repeat customers with discounts, exclusive offers, and special perks. This encourages continued patronage and demonstrates appreciation for their business.

Conclusion

Delivering exceptional customer service is fundamental to the success of your car dealership. By personalizing interactions, maintaining transparent communication, creating a welcoming environment, training and empowering staff, effectively handling complaints, and going the extra mile, you can build strong customer relationships, foster loyalty, and differentiate your dealership from the competition. In the next chapters, we'll explore leadership principles, operational excellence, financial management, and marketing innovations—all essential components for achieving long-term success in automotive retail.

Chapter 19: Effective Inventory Management

Welcome to Chapter 19 of your comprehensive guide on managing a successful car dealership! In this chapter, we'll explore the crucial aspects of inventory management, including best practices for maintaining optimal inventory levels, utilizing technology, and implementing strategies that ensure your dealership meets customer demands while minimizing costs.

Importance of Inventory Management

Meeting Customer Demand

Effective inventory management ensures that your dealership has the right vehicles in stock to meet customer demands. Having the right mix of vehicles, including new models, popular makes, and diverse options, increases the likelihood of making sales and satisfying customers.

Reducing Costs

Proper inventory management helps reduce holding costs, minimize depreciation, and avoid the financial burden of overstocking. Balancing inventory levels optimizes your cash flow and maximizes profitability.

Key Inventory Management Practices

Accurate Forecasting

- **Sales Data Analysis**: Utilize historical sales data to forecast future demand accurately. Analyze trends, seasonal fluctuations, and market conditions to predict which vehicles will be in demand.
- **Market Research**: Conduct market research to understand consumer preferences, emerging trends, and competitor offerings. Adjust your inventory based on these insights to stay ahead of the competition.

Inventory Turnover

- **Turnover Ratio**: Monitor your inventory turnover ratio to gauge how quickly vehicles are sold and replaced. A high turnover ratio indicates efficient inventory management, while a low ratio suggests overstocking or slow sales.
- **Aging Inventory**: Regularly review aging inventory to identify vehicles that have been on the lot for an extended period. Implement strategies to move these vehicles, such as offering discounts, promotions, or special financing options.

Utilizing Technology

Inventory Management Software

- **Automated Systems**: Implement inventory management software that automates tracking, ordering, and reporting processes. These systems provide real-time data on inventory levels, sales performance, and market trends, enabling informed decision-making.
- **Integration**: Integrate your inventory management software with other dealership systems, such as CRM and accounting software, to streamline operations and ensure data consistency across departments.

Online Platforms

- **Digital Listings**: Maintain up-to-date digital listings on your dealership's website and third-party platforms. High-quality photos, detailed descriptions, and accurate pricing information attract online shoppers and drive traffic to your dealership.
- **Virtual Showroom**: Create a virtual showroom experience using 360-degree photos and videos. Allow customers to explore vehicles online, view features, and schedule test drives, enhancing their shopping experience.

Inventory Sourcing and Acquisition

Diversified Sourcing

- **Manufacturer Relationships**: Build strong relationships with vehicle manufacturers to secure a steady supply of new models and negotiate favorable terms. Stay informed about upcoming releases and exclusive allocations.
- **Auction Participation**: Participate in vehicle auctions to acquire quality used vehicles at competitive prices. Ensure thorough inspection and verification processes to avoid purchasing problematic vehicles.

Trade-In Programs

- **Incentivize Trade-Ins**: Offer attractive trade-in programs to encourage customers to exchange their old vehicles for new ones. Provide competitive appraisals and streamline the trade-in process to enhance customer satisfaction.
- **Certified Pre-Owned**: Develop a certified pre-owned (CPO) program to offer high-quality used vehicles with extended warranties and rigorous inspections. CPO programs attract buyers seeking value and reliability.

Inventory Control and Optimization

Lot Organization

- **Efficient Layout**: Organize your dealership lot to maximize visibility and accessibility. Group similar vehicles together, create designated areas for new and used cars, and ensure easy navigation for customers.
- **Showroom Display**: Showcase high-demand vehicles and new arrivals prominently in your showroom. Use attractive displays, lighting, and signage to draw attention and create a compelling shopping experience.

Inventory Audits

- **Regular Audits**: Conduct regular inventory audits to verify stock levels, identify discrepancies, and ensure data accuracy. Audits help prevent theft, loss, and administrative errors.
- **Reconciliation**: Reconcile physical inventory with system records to maintain consistency. Address discrepancies promptly and implement corrective actions to prevent recurrence.

Strategies for Slow-Moving Inventory

Promotions and Discounts

- **Special Offers**: Create limited-time promotions and discounts for slow-moving inventory. Highlight these deals through marketing campaigns, both online and offline, to attract budget-conscious buyers.
- **Bundling**: Bundle slow-moving vehicles with popular accessories or services to increase their appeal. Offer packages that provide added value to customers while moving less desirable stock.

Conclusion

Effective inventory management is essential for maintaining optimal stock levels, meeting customer demand, and maximizing profitability in the automotive retail industry. By implementing accurate forecasting, utilizing technology, optimizing sourcing and acquisition, controlling inventory, and strategically addressing slow-moving stock, your dealership can achieve operational excellence and drive sales growth. In the next chapters, we'll explore leadership principles, financial management, marketing innovations, and customer service strategies—all critical components for building a resilient and successful automotive retail business.

Chapter 20: Financial Management for Automotive Dealerships

Welcome to Chapter 20 of your comprehensive guide on managing a successful car dealership! In this chapter, we'll delve into the fundamentals of financial management, focusing on strategies to ensure your dealership's profitability, sustainability, and growth. From budgeting and cash flow management to financial analysis and cost control, we'll cover essential practices that can help you navigate the financial landscape of the automotive industry.

Importance of Financial Management

Ensuring Profitability

Effective financial management ensures that your dealership remains profitable. By closely monitoring revenues, expenses, and profits, you can make informed decisions that enhance financial performance and business sustainability.

Facilitating Growth

Sound financial practices enable your dealership to invest in growth opportunities, such as expanding your inventory, upgrading facilities, or launching new marketing campaigns. Financial stability also makes it easier to secure loans and attract investors.

Budgeting and Planning

Creating a Comprehensive Budget

- **Revenue Projections**: Estimate your dealership's revenue based on historical sales data, market trends, and economic conditions. Consider different revenue streams, such as new and used vehicle sales, financing, and service departments.
- **Expense Management**: Identify and categorize all potential expenses, including salaries, utilities, rent, marketing, inventory

purchases, and maintenance. Allocate funds to each category and monitor spending to stay within budget.

Setting Financial Goals

- **Short-Term Goals**: Establish short-term financial goals, such as monthly or quarterly sales targets, expense reduction objectives, and profitability benchmarks. These goals help you track progress and make necessary adjustments.
- **Long-Term Goals**: Develop long-term financial goals, such as expanding to new locations, increasing market share, or achieving specific profitability margins. Long-term planning provides direction and focus for your dealership's growth.

Cash Flow Management

Importance of Cash Flow

- **Operational Stability**: Maintaining positive cash flow ensures that your dealership can meet its financial obligations, such as paying suppliers, employees, and other operational expenses. It prevents liquidity issues that can disrupt business operations.
- **Investment Opportunities**: Healthy cash flow enables you to take advantage of investment opportunities, such as purchasing high-demand inventory, investing in technology, or launching marketing campaigns to drive sales.

Cash Flow Strategies

- **Receivables Management**: Monitor and manage accounts receivable to ensure timely collections. Implement clear credit policies, offer incentives for early payments, and follow up on overdue accounts to improve cash flow.
- **Inventory Control**: Maintain optimal inventory levels to avoid tying up excessive capital in unsold vehicles. Use data analytics to forecast demand accurately and adjust inventory purchasing accordingly.

Financial Analysis and Reporting

Key Financial Statements

- **Income Statement**: The income statement provides an overview of your dealership's revenues, expenses, and profits over a specific period. Analyzing this statement helps you understand your profitability and identify areas for improvement.
- **Balance Sheet**: The balance sheet presents your dealership's assets, liabilities, and equity at a given point in time. It offers insights into your financial stability, liquidity, and overall financial health.
- **Cash Flow Statement**: The cash flow statement tracks the flow of cash in and out of your dealership. It highlights operating, investing, and financing activities, providing a comprehensive view of your cash position.

Financial Ratios

- **Gross Profit Margin**: The gross profit margin measures the difference between sales and the cost of goods sold (COGS). A higher margin indicates better profitability and cost management.
- **Current Ratio**: The current ratio compares your dealership's current assets to its current liabilities. A ratio above 1 indicates good liquidity, meaning you can cover short-term obligations.
- **Return on Investment (ROI)**: ROI measures the profitability of investments or business initiatives. It helps you evaluate the effectiveness of your spending and investment decisions.

Cost Control and Efficiency

Expense Monitoring

- **Regular Reviews**: Conduct regular reviews of all expenses to identify areas where costs can be reduced without

compromising quality. Analyze variances between actual expenses and budgeted amounts to uncover inefficiencies.
- **Vendor Negotiations**: Negotiate with suppliers and service providers to secure better terms, discounts, or bulk purchasing deals. Building strong relationships with vendors can lead to cost savings and improved service.

Process Optimization

- **Operational Efficiency**: Streamline dealership operations to reduce waste, improve productivity, and lower costs. Implement best practices, leverage technology, and train employees to work efficiently.
- **Energy Management**: Adopt energy-efficient practices to reduce utility costs. This might include using energy-efficient lighting, optimizing heating and cooling systems, and implementing a comprehensive energy management plan.

Conclusion

Effective financial management is the backbone of a successful car dealership. By creating comprehensive budgets, managing cash flow, analyzing financial statements, controlling costs, and setting clear financial goals, you can ensure your dealership's profitability and growth. Financial stability allows you to invest in new opportunities, weather economic challenges, and build a sustainable business. In the next chapters, we'll explore leadership principles, marketing innovations, customer service strategies, and more—critical components for achieving long-term success in the automotive retail industry.

Chapter 21: Leadership Principles for Automotive Dealerships

Welcome to Chapter 21 of your comprehensive guide on managing a successful car dealership! In this chapter, we'll explore the essential leadership principles that can guide you in effectively leading and inspiring your dealership team. Whether you're a seasoned dealer or new to the automotive industry, strong leadership is crucial for fostering a positive work culture, driving performance, and achieving long-term success.

The Role of Leadership in Automotive Retail

Vision and Strategy

Effective leadership begins with a clear vision and strategic direction for your dealership. Define your dealership's mission, goals, and values, and communicate them clearly to your team. A compelling vision inspires employees, aligns their efforts, and guides decision-making.

Team Building and Motivation

- **Building a Winning Team**: Surround yourself with talented individuals who share your vision and complement your strengths. Invest in recruiting, training, and retaining top talent across sales, service, finance, and administrative roles.
- **Employee Engagement**: Foster a culture of engagement and empowerment where employees feel valued, respected, and motivated to perform at their best. Encourage open communication, recognize achievements, and provide opportunities for professional growth.

Effective Communication

Transparent and Open Communication

- **Clear Expectations**: Set clear expectations for performance, behavior, and goals. Ensure that every team member

understands their responsibilities and how their contributions impact dealership success.
- **Listening and Feedback**: Practice active listening to understand employee concerns, ideas, and feedback. Create opportunities for open dialogue and constructive feedback sessions to foster continuous improvement.

Strategic Decision-Making

Data-Driven Decisions

- **Utilizing Data**: Leverage data analytics and market insights to make informed decisions about inventory management, pricing strategies, marketing campaigns, and customer service initiatives. Monitor key performance indicators (KPIs) to track progress and adjust strategies as needed.
- **Risk Management**: Anticipate potential challenges and risks in the automotive industry, such as economic fluctuations, regulatory changes, and market competition. Develop contingency plans and mitigate risks through proactive measures.

Leading by Example

Integrity and Ethics

- **Ethical Leadership**: Demonstrate integrity, honesty, and ethical behavior in all business dealings. Uphold high standards of professionalism, compliance with industry regulations, and respect for customers, employees, and stakeholders.
- **Customer-Centric Focus**: Prioritize customer satisfaction and loyalty by delivering exceptional service, maintaining transparency, and resolving issues promptly and fairly. Lead by example in creating a customer-centric culture.

Innovation and Adaptability

Embracing Change

- **Innovative Thinking**: Encourage a culture of innovation and continuous improvement. Embrace new technologies, trends, and industry innovations to stay ahead of competitors and meet evolving customer expectations.
- **Adaptability**: Be flexible and adaptable in responding to market shifts, consumer preferences, and industry disruptions. Empower your team to embrace change and proactively seek opportunities for growth and innovation.

Leadership Development

Investing in Growth

- **Continuous Learning**: Invest in leadership development programs, workshops, and industry certifications to enhance your leadership skills and business acumen. Stay updated on industry trends, best practices, and leadership strategies.
- **Mentorship and Coaching**: Provide mentorship and coaching to emerging leaders within your dealership. Foster a pipeline of talent by nurturing future leaders and preparing them for increased responsibilities.

Building Relationships

Stakeholder Management

- **Partnerships and Collaborations**: Build strong relationships with manufacturers, suppliers, financial institutions, and community stakeholders. Collaborate on joint ventures, promotional campaigns, and community outreach initiatives to strengthen your dealership's reputation and market presence.
- **Networking**: Attend automotive industry events, conferences, and networking opportunities to build industry connections, exchange ideas, and stay informed about industry developments.

Conclusion

Effective leadership is fundamental to the success and sustainability of your car dealership. By establishing a compelling vision, building a talented team, fostering open communication, making data-driven decisions, leading by example, embracing innovation, investing in leadership development, and cultivating strong relationships, you can create a culture of excellence and drive performance across your dealership. In the next chapters, we'll explore operational excellence, financial management, marketing innovations, customer service strategies, and more—essential components for achieving long-term success in the dynamic automotive retail industry.

Chapter 22: Achieving Operational Excellence in Your Car Dealership

Welcome to Chapter 22 of your guide on managing a successful car dealership! In this chapter, we will delve into the principles and strategies for achieving operational excellence. Operational excellence is about optimizing processes, maximizing efficiency, and delivering exceptional value to customers. By implementing effective operational practices, you can streamline workflows, improve customer satisfaction, and drive profitability in your dealership.

Importance of Operational Excellence

Enhancing Efficiency

Operational excellence focuses on streamlining operations and reducing waste, which leads to improved efficiency throughout your dealership. Efficient processes save time, minimize costs, and enhance overall productivity.

Customer Satisfaction

Efficient operations contribute to a positive customer experience by ensuring timely service, accurate information, and smooth transactions. Satisfied customers are more likely to return for future purchases and recommend your dealership to others.

Process Optimization

Lean Principles

- **Identifying Waste**: Apply lean principles to identify and eliminate waste in processes, such as overproduction, unnecessary waiting times, excess inventory, and inefficient workflows. Streamline operations to deliver value to customers with minimal resources.
- **Continuous Improvement**: Foster a culture of continuous improvement where employees are encouraged to identify

inefficiencies, suggest improvements, and implement changes that enhance productivity and customer satisfaction.

Inventory Management

Optimizing Inventory Levels

- **Demand Forecasting**: Use historical sales data, market trends, and customer preferences to forecast demand accurately. Maintain optimal inventory levels to meet customer needs without overstocking or understocking vehicles.
- **Just-in-Time (JIT) Inventory**: Implement JIT principles to reduce inventory holding costs and improve inventory turnover rates. Coordinate closely with suppliers to ensure timely vehicle deliveries based on customer demand.

Operational Efficiency in Sales

Sales Process Optimization

- **Customer Relationship Management (CRM)**: Utilize CRM software to manage customer interactions, track leads, and nurture relationships throughout the sales process. Personalize communications and follow up with prospects to increase conversion rates.
- **Sales Training**: Provide comprehensive sales training to equip your sales team with product knowledge, negotiation skills, and customer service techniques. Empower them to deliver a seamless buying experience and exceed customer expectations.

Service Department Excellence

Enhancing Service Operations

- **Appointment Scheduling**: Implement efficient scheduling systems to minimize wait times and optimize service bay

utilization. Offer online appointment booking options for convenience and accessibility.
- **Quality Assurance**: Establish rigorous quality assurance protocols to ensure service excellence and customer satisfaction. Conduct regular inspections, performance evaluations, and customer feedback surveys to maintain high standards.

Technology Integration

Leveraging Automotive Technology

- **Digital Tools**: Invest in automotive software solutions for inventory management, CRM, service scheduling, and financial reporting. Leverage data analytics to gain insights into customer behavior, market trends, and operational performance.
- **Customer Engagement Platforms**: Use digital platforms, such as your dealership's website and mobile apps, to engage customers, showcase inventory, facilitate online purchases, and provide personalized service recommendations.

Employee Engagement and Training

Empowering Your Team

- **Training and Development**: Invest in ongoing training and development programs to enhance employee skills, product knowledge, and customer service capabilities. Equip your team with the tools and resources they need to succeed.
- **Empowerment**: Empower employees to take ownership of their roles, make informed decisions, and resolve customer issues proactively. Foster a collaborative environment where teamwork and innovation thrive.

Quality Management

Ensuring High Standards

- **Quality Control Processes**: Implement robust quality control processes across all dealership operations, from vehicle inspections and maintenance to customer service interactions. Maintain consistency and reliability in service delivery.
- **Feedback Mechanisms**: Solicit feedback from customers through surveys, reviews, and direct communication. Use insights to identify areas for improvement, address customer concerns promptly, and continuously elevate service quality.

Conclusion

Achieving operational excellence requires a strategic focus on efficiency, customer satisfaction, process optimization, technology integration, employee engagement, and quality management. By implementing these principles and strategies, your car dealership can enhance operational performance, differentiate itself in the competitive automotive market, and sustain long-term success. In the next chapters, we'll explore financial management, marketing innovations, customer service strategies, leadership principles, and more—essential components for building a resilient and thriving automotive retail business.

Chapter 23: Marketing Strategies for Automotive Dealerships

Welcome to Chapter 23 of your guide on managing a successful car dealership! In this chapter, we'll explore effective marketing strategies tailored specifically for automotive dealerships. A robust marketing strategy is essential for attracting customers, increasing brand awareness, and driving sales in the competitive automotive industry. Whether you're looking to promote new models, boost service department bookings, or enhance customer engagement, implementing targeted marketing tactics can help your dealership thrive.

Understanding Your Market

Market Segmentation

- **Identifying Target Audience**: Define your dealership's target market based on demographic factors (age, income, location), psychographic traits (lifestyle, preferences), and behavioral patterns (buying habits, vehicle preferences). Tailor your marketing efforts to resonate with specific customer segments.
- **Competitive Analysis**: Conduct a thorough analysis of competitors' marketing strategies, pricing models, and customer engagement tactics. Identify gaps and opportunities to differentiate your dealership and attract new customers.

Digital Marketing Strategies

Online Presence

- **Website Optimization**: Ensure your dealership's website is user-friendly, mobile-responsive, and optimized for search engines (SEO). Include detailed vehicle listings, customer testimonials, service information, and easy-to-find contact details.
- **Search Engine Marketing (SEM)**: Launch targeted pay-per-click (PPC) advertising campaigns on search engines like Google. Use relevant keywords (e.g., "new car dealership near [location]") to

drive traffic to your website and capture leads actively searching for vehicles.

Social Media Marketing

- **Engaging Content**: Share engaging content on social media platforms (e.g., Facebook, Instagram, Twitter) to showcase inventory, highlight promotions, and engage with followers. Use visuals, videos, and customer testimonials to capture attention and build brand credibility.
- **Community Engagement**: Foster community engagement by participating in local events, sponsoring charity initiatives, and sharing dealership news and activities. Build relationships with local influencers and community organizations to enhance brand visibility.

Content Marketing

Educational Content

- **Blog Posts and Articles**: Publish informative blog posts, articles, and how-to guides related to car buying tips, maintenance advice, industry trends, and vehicle reviews. Position your dealership as a trusted resource and attract organic traffic from search engines.
- **Video Marketing**: Create engaging video content, such as virtual vehicle tours, customer testimonials, and behind-the-scenes dealership tours. Leverage platforms like YouTube and social media to reach a broader audience and showcase your dealership's offerings.

Email Marketing Campaigns

Targeted Campaigns

- **Customer Segmentation**: Segment your email list based on customer preferences, purchase history, and service needs.

Send personalized email campaigns with relevant content, special offers, and dealership updates to nurture leads and encourage repeat business.
- **Automated Follow-Ups**: Set up automated email workflows to follow up with leads, send appointment reminders, and gather customer feedback. Use email marketing analytics to measure campaign effectiveness and refine your messaging strategies.

Customer Relationship Management (CRM)

Building Relationships

- **Personalized Communication**: Use CRM software to track customer interactions, preferences, and purchase history. Send personalized messages on birthdays, anniversaries, and vehicle milestones to strengthen customer relationships and encourage loyalty.
- **Referral Programs**: Implement referral programs that reward customers for recommending your dealership to friends and family. Offer incentives, such as discounts on services or accessories, to encourage referrals and generate new leads.

Traditional Marketing Tactics

Local Advertising

- **Print Advertising**: Place advertisements in local newspapers, magazines, and automotive publications to reach a targeted audience. Include compelling visuals, promotional offers, and dealership contact information to attract potential customers.
- **Direct Mail Campaigns**: Launch direct mail campaigns targeting specific geographic areas or customer segments. Send postcards, brochures, and promotional offers to prospects and past customers to drive traffic to your dealership.

Measuring Success

Analytics and Reporting

- **Key Performance Indicators (KPIs)**: Monitor KPIs such as website traffic, lead conversion rates, social media engagement, and return on investment (ROI) from marketing campaigns. Use analytics tools to track performance, identify trends, and optimize marketing strategies.
- **Customer Feedback**: Solicit feedback from customers through surveys, reviews, and social media interactions. Use insights to refine marketing messages, improve customer experience, and address areas for enhancement.

Conclusion

Effective marketing strategies are essential for attracting prospective customers, enhancing brand visibility, and driving sales growth in the competitive automotive industry. By understanding your target market, leveraging digital marketing channels, creating engaging content, nurturing customer relationships, and measuring campaign effectiveness, your dealership can achieve marketing success and establish a strong market presence. In the next chapters, we'll explore customer service strategies, operational excellence, financial management, leadership principles, and more—critical components for building a resilient and thriving automotive retail business.

Chapter 24: Customer Service Strategies for Automotive Dealerships

Welcome to Chapter 24 of your comprehensive guide on managing a successful car dealership! In this chapter, we'll delve into the importance of customer service and explore effective strategies for delivering exceptional customer experiences in the automotive industry. Customer service is not just about resolving issues; it's about building relationships, earning trust, and fostering loyalty among your customers. By prioritizing customer satisfaction and implementing proactive service initiatives, your dealership can differentiate itself, drive repeat business, and achieve long-term success.

The Importance of Customer Service

Building Trust and Loyalty

Customer service plays a pivotal role in building trust and loyalty with your dealership's clientele. Positive interactions, timely assistance, and personalized attention create memorable experiences that influence customer perception and retention.

Reputation Management

Exceptional customer service contributes to a positive reputation for your dealership. Satisfied customers are more likely to recommend your services to others, leave positive reviews, and contribute to your dealership's growth through word-of-mouth referrals.

Creating a Customer-Centric Culture

Leadership Commitment

- **Leadership Role**: Demonstrate a commitment to customer service excellence from the top down. Emphasize the importance of customer satisfaction in dealership operations and empower employees to prioritize customer needs.

- **Training and Development**: Provide comprehensive training programs to equip employees with the skills, knowledge, and empathy needed to deliver outstanding customer service. Role-playing exercises and real-world scenarios can enhance their ability to handle diverse customer interactions.

Effective Communication

Listening and Understanding

- **Active Listening**: Practice active listening to understand customers' concerns, preferences, and expectations. Encourage open dialogue and ask probing questions to clarify issues and demonstrate genuine interest in resolving them.
- **Clear Communication**: Communicate information clearly and concisely, whether discussing vehicle features, service recommendations, pricing, or dealership policies. Use plain language and avoid jargon to ensure understanding.

Personalized Service Experience

Tailoring Services

- **Customer Preferences**: Take note of customers' preferences and past interactions to personalize their service experience. Remember details such as preferred communication channels, vehicle preferences, and service history to enhance rapport.
- **Customized Recommendations**: Provide personalized recommendations based on customers' needs and vehicle requirements. Offer options for accessories, maintenance packages, and upgrades that align with their preferences and driving habits.

Service Department Excellence

Timeliness and Efficiency

- **Appointment Scheduling**: Implement efficient appointment scheduling systems to minimize wait times and optimize service bay utilization. Offer online booking options and send reminders to streamline the customer experience.
- **Service Transparency**: Maintain transparency throughout the service process by keeping customers informed about service progress, anticipated timelines, and any additional repairs or costs. Proactively address any unexpected issues that arise.

Resolving Issues and Complaints

Effective Problem Resolution

- **Prompt Response**: Respond promptly to customer inquiries, complaints, and service requests. Acknowledge issues with empathy, investigate thoroughly, and provide clear resolutions or alternatives to restore customer confidence.
- **Feedback Mechanisms**: Encourage customers to provide feedback through surveys, reviews, and direct interactions. Use feedback to identify areas for improvement, address recurring issues, and enhance service delivery.

Building Long-Term Relationships

Follow-Up and Engagement

- **Post-Service Follow-Up**: Follow up with customers after service appointments to ensure satisfaction and address any lingering concerns. Express gratitude for their business and invite them to provide feedback on their experience.
- **Customer Loyalty Programs**: Implement customer loyalty programs that reward repeat business and referrals. Offer incentives such as discounts on future services, exclusive promotions, or VIP benefits to cultivate long-term relationships.

Leveraging Technology

Enhancing Service Efficiency

- **CRM Systems**: Utilize customer relationship management (CRM) systems to maintain detailed customer profiles, track service histories, and automate personalized communications. Leverage data analytics to anticipate customer needs and preferences.
- **Digital Tools**: Integrate digital tools, such as online appointment scheduling, service reminders, and mobile apps, to enhance convenience and accessibility for customers. Provide self-service options for vehicle status updates and service approvals.

Measuring Customer Satisfaction

Performance Metrics

- **Customer Satisfaction Surveys**: Conduct regular customer satisfaction surveys to gauge service quality, identify strengths and areas for improvement, and benchmark against industry standards. Use Net Promoter Score (NPS) and customer feedback ratings to measure loyalty and advocacy.
- **Service Quality Indicators**: Monitor service quality indicators, such as service completion times, first-time fix rates, and customer wait times. Set performance goals and track progress to continuously elevate service standards.

Conclusion

Delivering exceptional customer service is fundamental to the success and sustainability of your car dealership. By fostering a customer-centric culture, prioritizing effective communication, personalizing service experiences, optimizing service department operations, resolving issues promptly, building long-term relationships, leveraging technology, and measuring customer satisfaction, your dealership can establish a reputation for excellence and achieve competitive advantage. In the next chapters, we'll explore operational excellence, financial management, marketing strategies, leadership principles, and more—essential components for building a resilient and customer-focused automotive retail business.

Building Trust and Loyalty

Customer service is about more than solving problems; it's about building relationships. Consistently positive interactions make customers feel valued and respected, fostering trust and loyalty. A loyal customer base will not only return for future purchases but will also recommend your dealership to others.

Enhancing Reputation

Word-of-mouth referrals are powerful in the automotive industry. Exceptional customer service leads to positive reviews and recommendations, enhancing your dealership's reputation. Conversely, poor service can quickly damage your reputation and deter potential customers.

Creating a Customer-Centric Culture

Leadership Commitment

- **Lead by Example**: As a leader, demonstrate a commitment to customer service. Your actions set the tone for the rest of the team. Show that customer satisfaction is a top priority by being involved and responsive.
- **Invest in Training**: Provide ongoing training for your staff to ensure they have the skills and knowledge to deliver excellent service. Training should cover product knowledge, communication skills, and problem-solving techniques.

Effective Communication

Listening and Understanding

- **Active Listening**: Encourage your team to practice active listening. This means fully concentrating on the customer, understanding their needs, responding appropriately, and remembering key details.

- **Empathy and Understanding**: Train your staff to show empathy. Understanding and acknowledging a customer's feelings and perspectives can turn a potentially negative situation into a positive experience.

Clear and Concise Communication

- **Clarity**: Ensure that all communications, whether in person, over the phone, or online, are clear and easy to understand. Avoid jargon and ensure that customers fully understand the information provided.
- **Follow-Up**: Always follow up with customers after a sale or service appointment. This shows that you care about their experience and are committed to their satisfaction.

Personalized Service

Knowing Your Customers

- **Customer Profiles**: Use customer relationship management (CRM) systems to maintain detailed profiles of your customers. This includes their vehicle preferences, purchase history, and service records.
- **Tailored Recommendations**: Use the information from your CRM to provide personalized service. For example, recommend service packages based on their vehicle's history or suggest new models that fit their preferences.

Special Touches

- **Personalized Communication**: Send personalized emails or messages to acknowledge birthdays, anniversaries, or vehicle purchase anniversaries. Small gestures like these can make a big difference in how customers perceive your dealership.
- **Exclusive Offers**: Provide exclusive offers or promotions to loyal customers. This makes them feel valued and appreciated.

Efficient Service Department

Timeliness and Transparency

- **Appointment Scheduling**: Make scheduling service appointments easy and convenient. Offer online booking and flexible time slots to accommodate customers' schedules.
- **Transparency**: Keep customers informed throughout the service process. Explain the work that will be done, provide accurate estimates, and notify them of any changes.

Quality Assurance

- **Attention to Detail**: Ensure that all work is completed to the highest standards. Double-check that every task is done correctly and that the vehicle is returned in pristine condition.
- **Feedback Collection**: After service, solicit feedback from customers to understand their experience and identify areas for improvement.

Handling Complaints and Issues

Proactive Problem Solving

- **Address Issues Promptly**: When a complaint arises, address it quickly and efficiently. The faster you resolve a problem, the more likely the customer is to be satisfied.
- **Empower Employees**: Empower your employees to make decisions that can resolve issues on the spot. This reduces wait times for customers and demonstrates your commitment to their satisfaction.

Learning from Feedback

- **Analyze Feedback**: Regularly review customer feedback to identify common issues and trends. Use this information to make systematic improvements to your processes and services.

- **Continuous Improvement**: Foster a culture of continuous improvement. Encourage your team to always look for ways to enhance the customer experience.

Conclusion

Delivering exceptional customer service is fundamental to the success and sustainability of your car dealership. By fostering a customer-centric culture, prioritizing effective communication, personalizing service experiences, optimizing service department operations, resolving issues promptly, and leveraging technology, your dealership can establish a reputation for excellence and achieve a competitive advantage. In the next chapters, we'll explore operational excellence, financial management, marketing strategies, leadership principles, and more—critical components for building a resilient and thriving automotive retail business.

Chapter 25: Financial Management for Automotive Dealerships

Welcome to Chapter 25 of your comprehensive guide on managing a successful car dealership! In this chapter, we'll dive into the critical aspects of financial management. Understanding and effectively managing your dealership's finances is key to sustaining profitability, making informed business decisions, and ensuring long-term success. We'll cover essential financial principles, budgeting, cost control, revenue management, and strategies for maximizing profitability.

The Importance of Financial Management

Sustaining Profitability

Effective financial management ensures that your dealership remains profitable. By keeping track of income and expenses, you can identify trends, optimize operations, and make strategic decisions that boost your bottom line.

Informed Decision-Making

Accurate financial data provides a clear picture of your dealership's performance. It helps you make informed decisions about inventory purchases, marketing investments, staffing, and expansion opportunities.

Setting Up a Financial Management System

Accounting Basics

- **Chart of Accounts**: Create a detailed chart of accounts to categorize all financial transactions. This helps in tracking and managing income, expenses, assets, liabilities, and equity.
- **Double-Entry Bookkeeping**: Use double-entry bookkeeping to maintain accurate records. Each transaction should be recorded in at least two accounts (debit and credit) to ensure the books are balanced.

Financial Statements

- **Income Statement**: Also known as the profit and loss statement, this report shows your dealership's revenues, expenses, and profits over a specific period. It helps assess profitability and operational efficiency.
- **Balance Sheet**: This statement provides a snapshot of your dealership's financial position at a given point in time. It lists assets, liabilities, and equity, showing what you own and owe.
- **Cash Flow Statement**: This report details cash inflows and outflows, helping you understand how money is being generated and spent. It's crucial for managing liquidity and ensuring you have enough cash to meet obligations.

Budgeting and Forecasting

Creating a Budget

- **Revenue Projections**: Estimate your dealership's revenues based on historical data, market trends, and sales goals. Consider all income sources, including vehicle sales, service department, and financing.
- **Expense Planning**: List all expected expenses, including fixed costs (rent, salaries) and variable costs (inventory, marketing). Allocate funds accordingly and ensure expenses don't exceed revenues.

Financial Forecasting

- **Scenario Analysis**: Conduct scenario analysis to prepare for different financial outcomes. Create best-case, worst-case, and most-likely scenarios to understand potential impacts on your dealership's finances.
- **Regular Reviews**: Regularly review and adjust your budget based on actual performance and changing market conditions. This helps in staying on track and making necessary adjustments promptly.

Cost Control and Efficiency

Managing Operating Costs

- **Inventory Management**: Optimize inventory levels to reduce holding costs and avoid overstocking. Use data analytics to forecast demand and adjust inventory accordingly.
- **Supplier Negotiations**: Negotiate favorable terms with suppliers for better pricing, discounts, and payment terms. Building strong relationships can lead to cost savings.

Reducing Overhead

- **Energy Efficiency**: Implement energy-efficient practices to reduce utility bills. Use energy-saving lighting, optimize heating and cooling systems, and encourage eco-friendly practices among staff.
- **Technology Utilization**: Invest in technology that streamlines operations and reduces manual labor. For example, use dealership management systems (DMS) to automate administrative tasks and improve efficiency.

Revenue Management

Diversifying Income Streams

- **Service Department**: Maximize revenue from the service department by offering maintenance packages, extended warranties, and upselling services. Ensure high service quality to build customer loyalty.
- **Finance and Insurance (F&I)**: Enhance your F&I offerings by providing competitive financing options, insurance products, and protection plans. Train your staff to effectively present these options to customers.

Sales Strategies

- **Pricing Strategies**: Implement dynamic pricing strategies based on market demand, competition, and inventory levels. Offer promotions and incentives to attract customers and boost sales.
- **Sales Training**: Invest in ongoing sales training to enhance your team's skills in closing deals, upselling, and customer relationship management. A well-trained sales team can significantly increase revenue.

Monitoring Financial Performance

Key Performance Indicators (KPIs)

- **Gross Profit Margin**: Monitor the gross profit margin on vehicle sales and services. This indicator shows how efficiently you are generating profit from your core operations.
- **Net Profit Margin**: Track the net profit margin to understand overall profitability after all expenses. Aim to improve this metric by increasing revenues and controlling costs.
- **Inventory Turnover**: Measure how quickly inventory is sold and replaced. A higher turnover rate indicates efficient inventory management and strong sales performance.

Regular Financial Reviews

- **Monthly Reports**: Conduct monthly financial reviews to assess performance against budget and identify areas for improvement. Use these insights to make informed decisions and adjust strategies.
- **Annual Audits**: Perform annual audits to ensure financial accuracy and compliance with regulations. Audits provide an opportunity to identify discrepancies, strengthen controls, and enhance transparency.

Conclusion

Effective financial management is the cornerstone of a successful automotive dealership. By setting up a robust financial system, budgeting wisely, controlling costs, managing revenues, and monitoring performance, you can ensure your dealership remains profitable and competitive. In the next chapters, we'll explore marketing strategies, customer service excellence, leadership principles, and more—essential components for building a resilient and thriving automotive retail business.

Chapter 26: Leadership Principles for Automotive Dealerships

Welcome to Chapter 26 of your guide on managing a successful car dealership! In this chapter, we'll explore essential leadership principles tailored for automotive dealership owners and managers. Effective leadership is crucial for guiding your dealership towards success, inspiring your team, fostering a positive work environment, and achieving organizational goals. Whether you're a seasoned leader or aspiring to enhance your leadership skills, understanding these principles can empower you to lead with confidence and drive excellence in your dealership.

The Role of Leadership in Automotive Dealerships

Vision and Strategy

As a leader, it's essential to articulate a clear vision for your dealership's future. Your vision should inspire and guide your team, aligning everyone towards common objectives. Develop strategic plans that outline goals, milestones, and actionable steps to achieve success.

Inspiring and Motivating Teams

- **Effective Communication**: Communicate openly and transparently with your team. Share the dealership's vision, goals, and expectations clearly. Encourage feedback and collaboration to foster a supportive environment.
- **Recognition and Appreciation**: Recognize and appreciate your team's contributions regularly. Celebrate achievements, milestones, and individual successes. Acknowledging hard work boosts morale and encourages continued dedication.

Building a Positive Organizational Culture

Values and Ethics

- **Lead by Example**: Demonstrate integrity, honesty, and ethical behavior in all interactions. Uphold dealership values and set high standards for professionalism and customer service. Your actions will set the tone for the entire team.
- **Inclusivity and Diversity**: Foster an inclusive workplace culture that values diversity. Embrace different perspectives and ideas, creating a collaborative environment where every team member feels respected and valued.

Developing and Empowering Your Team

Training and Development

- **Invest in Training**: Provide ongoing training and development opportunities for your team. Equip them with the skills, knowledge, and resources needed to excel in their roles. Encourage continuous learning and professional growth.
- **Empowerment**: Delegate responsibilities and empower your team to make decisions autonomously within their roles. Trusting your team fosters confidence and initiative, driving innovation and efficiency.

Strategic Decision-Making

Data-Driven Insights

- **Utilize Data**: Leverage data analytics to make informed decisions. Analyze sales trends, customer preferences, and operational metrics to identify opportunities for improvement and optimize dealership performance.
- **Risk Management**: Assess risks associated with business decisions carefully. Develop contingency plans to mitigate risks and adapt quickly to changing market conditions or unforeseen challenges.

Customer-Centric Approach

Focus on Customer Experience

- **Customer Feedback**: Listen to customer feedback attentively. Use insights to enhance products, services, and dealership processes. Prioritize exceptional customer service to build loyalty and positive word-of-mouth.
- **Personalized Service**: Tailor interactions to meet individual customer needs and preferences. Create memorable experiences that exceed expectations and strengthen customer relationships.

Operational Excellence

Efficiency and Innovation

- **Process Optimization**: Streamline dealership operations to improve efficiency and reduce costs. Implement technology solutions, such as dealership management systems (DMS), to automate tasks and enhance productivity.
- **Continuous Improvement**: Foster a culture of continuous improvement. Encourage team members to identify inefficiencies, propose innovative solutions, and implement best practices to drive operational excellence.

Leading Through Challenges

Resilience and Adaptability

- **Stay Agile**: Navigate challenges and market fluctuations with resilience. Adapt strategies and operations as needed to maintain competitiveness and sustain dealership growth.
- **Team Support**: Support your team during challenging times. Provide guidance, encouragement, and resources to help them overcome obstacles and stay motivated.

Communication and Transparency

Open Dialogue

- **Transparent Communication**: Keep your team informed about dealership goals, performance metrics, and industry developments. Foster open communication channels where team members feel comfortable sharing ideas and concerns.
- **Feedback Mechanisms**: Implement regular feedback mechanisms to solicit input from your team. Act on feedback to address issues promptly and improve dealership operations continuously.

Leading by Example

Personal Growth

- **Self-Reflection**: Continuously evaluate your own leadership style and effectiveness. Seek feedback from mentors, peers, and team members to identify areas for improvement and refine your leadership approach.
- **Balance and Well-being**: Maintain a healthy work-life balance and prioritize well-being. A balanced leader sets a positive example and fosters a culture of wellness within the dealership.

Conclusion

Effective leadership is fundamental to the success and sustainability of your automotive dealership. By embodying vision, inspiring your team, cultivating a positive culture, developing talent, making strategic decisions, prioritizing customer experience, driving operational excellence, navigating challenges with resilience, fostering transparent communication, and leading by example, you can create a thriving dealership that excels in a competitive market. In the next chapters, we'll explore financial management, marketing strategies, customer service excellence, and more—essential components for building a resilient and customer-focused automotive retail business.

Chapter 27: Digital Marketing Strategies for Automotive Dealerships

Welcome to Chapter 27 of your comprehensive guide on managing a successful car dealership! In this chapter, we will explore effective digital marketing strategies tailored specifically for automotive dealerships. In today's digital age, leveraging online platforms and tools is essential for reaching potential customers, building brand awareness, and driving sales. Whether you're new to digital marketing or looking to refine your existing strategies, understanding these tactics will empower you to effectively navigate the digital landscape and achieve your dealership's marketing goals.

Importance of Digital Marketing for Automotive Dealerships

Reach and Engagement

Digital marketing enables your dealership to reach a broader audience beyond traditional advertising methods. By utilizing digital channels, you can engage with potential customers where they spend a significant amount of their time—online.

Brand Visibility and Awareness

Effective digital marketing increases your dealership's visibility and enhances brand awareness. Consistent online presence through various digital platforms helps to establish your dealership as a reputable and trusted choice among consumers.

Developing a Digital Marketing Strategy

Define Your Goals

- **Identify Objectives**: Determine specific goals for your digital marketing efforts, such as increasing website traffic, generating leads, boosting sales, or promoting new vehicle models. Clear objectives will guide your strategy and measure success.

Target Audience Identification

- **Customer Persona Development**: Create detailed customer personas based on demographic data, buying behavior, interests, and online habits. Understanding your target audience allows you to tailor marketing messages and strategies effectively.

Key Digital Marketing Channels and Strategies

Search Engine Optimization (SEO)

- **Optimize Website**: Enhance your dealership's website for search engines to improve organic visibility and attract more visitors. Focus on relevant keywords, high-quality content, mobile optimization, and user experience (UX).

Pay-Per-Click Advertising (PPC)

- **Google Ads**: Utilize Google Ads to bid on relevant keywords related to automotive sales and services. PPC campaigns can drive immediate traffic to your website and generate leads, especially for targeted promotions and seasonal offers.

Social Media Marketing

- **Platform Selection**: Choose social media platforms (e.g., Facebook, Instagram, Twitter) where your target audience is most active. Create engaging content, including vehicle showcases, customer testimonials, behind-the-scenes glimpses, and interactive polls.
- **Community Engagement**: Foster relationships with your audience through regular updates, responding to comments and messages promptly, and participating in relevant automotive discussions and forums.

Content Marketing

Valuable Content Creation

- **Blog Posts and Articles**: Publish informative and engaging blog posts on topics such as car maintenance tips, vehicle reviews, industry trends, and dealership news. Position your dealership as a knowledgeable resource within the automotive industry.
- **Video Marketing**: Leverage the power of video content to showcase vehicle features, virtual test drives, customer testimonials, and dealership events. Video engages viewers and can significantly influence purchasing decisions.

Email Marketing Campaigns

Targeted Communication

- **Segmented Campaigns**: Segment your email list based on customer preferences, purchase history, and engagement levels. Deliver personalized content, including promotional offers, service reminders, and exclusive dealership updates.
- **Automation Tools**: Use email marketing automation tools to schedule campaigns, track performance metrics (e.g., open rates, click-through rates), and nurture leads through automated workflows.

Online Reputation Management

Monitor and Respond

- **Customer Reviews**: Monitor online reviews on platforms like Google My Business, Yelp, and social media. Respond promptly to customer feedback, whether positive or negative, to demonstrate your dealership's commitment to customer satisfaction.
- **Brand Perception**: Manage your dealership's online reputation by addressing concerns, resolving issues proactively, and highlighting positive customer experiences. Positive reviews and testimonials can influence potential customers.

Analytics and Performance Measurement

Track and Evaluate

- **Data Analysis**: Utilize digital analytics tools (e.g., Google Analytics, social media insights) to measure the performance of your digital marketing campaigns. Monitor key metrics such as website traffic, conversion rates, lead generation, and return on investment (ROI).
- **Optimization Strategies**: Use data insights to optimize your marketing strategies continually. Adjust tactics based on performance data to maximize effectiveness and achieve marketing objectives more efficiently.

Compliance and Data Security

Adherence to Regulations

- **Privacy Policies**: Ensure compliance with data protection regulations (e.g., GDPR, CCPA) when collecting and using customer data for marketing purposes. Maintain transparency regarding data practices and customer consent.

Conclusion

Implementing effective digital marketing strategies is essential for automotive dealerships looking to expand their reach, increase brand visibility, and drive sales in today's competitive market. By developing a comprehensive digital marketing plan, leveraging SEO, PPC advertising, social media engagement, content marketing, email campaigns, managing online reputation, analyzing performance metrics, and ensuring compliance with data regulations, your dealership can effectively connect with prospective customers and build lasting relationships. In the next chapters, we'll explore customer service excellence, operational efficiency, leadership principles, and more—critical components for achieving sustained success in the automotive retail industry.

Chapter 28: Inventory Management Strategies for Automotive Dealerships

Welcome to Chapter 28 of your comprehensive guide on managing a successful car dealership! In this chapter, we will delve into effective inventory management strategies tailored specifically for automotive dealerships. Managing inventory efficiently is crucial for maximizing profitability, maintaining cash flow, meeting customer demand, and optimizing operational efficiency. Whether you're a new dealership owner or looking to refine your inventory management practices, understanding these strategies will empower you to streamline processes and achieve better results.

Importance of Inventory Management

Balance Between Supply and Demand

Effective inventory management ensures that your dealership maintains an optimal balance between vehicle supply and customer demand. It prevents overstocking, which ties up capital, and understocking, which leads to missed sales opportunities.

Customer Satisfaction

Having the right vehicles in stock ensures that you can meet customer preferences and expectations promptly. This enhances customer satisfaction, builds trust, and encourages repeat business and referrals.

Inventory Planning and Forecasting

Data-Driven Decision Making

- **Historical Sales Data**: Analyze historical sales trends to predict demand for different vehicle models, trim levels, and features. Use this data to stock vehicles that are popular in your market and adjust inventory levels accordingly.

- **Market Trends**: Stay informed about industry trends, consumer preferences, and competitor offerings. Monitor changes in demand for specific vehicle types (e.g., SUVs, electric vehicles) and adapt your inventory strategy accordingly.

Effective Inventory Management Practices

Categorization and Organization

- **Segmentation**: Categorize vehicles based on factors such as brand, model, type (e.g., new, certified pre-owned), and price range. Organize inventory in a way that facilitates easy access, inspection, and tracking.
- **Aging Inventory**: Monitor aging inventory regularly to identify vehicles that have been in stock for an extended period. Implement strategies such as price adjustments, promotions, or marketing campaigns to move aged inventory quickly.

Inventory Turnover and Holding Costs

Optimizing Turnover Rates

- **Inventory Turnover Ratio**: Calculate the inventory turnover ratio to measure how quickly vehicles are sold and replaced. Aim for a balance between high turnover rates to minimize holding costs and sufficient inventory to meet customer demand.
- **Reducing Holding Costs**: Minimize holding costs associated with unsold inventory by negotiating favorable terms with suppliers, optimizing storage space, and implementing efficient vehicle reconditioning processes.

Pricing and Merchandising Strategies

Competitive Pricing

- **Market Analysis**: Conduct regular market analysis to stay competitive with vehicle pricing. Monitor competitor pricing, consider market demand, and adjust pricing strategies accordingly to attract price-sensitive customers.
- **Transparent Pricing**: Maintain transparency in pricing to build trust with customers. Clearly display vehicle prices online and in-store, including any discounts, incentives, or additional fees.

Technology and Automation

Utilizing Dealership Management Systems (DMS)

- **Inventory Tracking**: Implement a DMS to track inventory levels, monitor vehicle movements, and manage vehicle acquisition and disposition processes efficiently. Utilize DMS features for real-time inventory updates and reporting.
- **Automated Reordering**: Use automation within your DMS to streamline vehicle reordering processes based on predefined inventory thresholds and sales forecasts. This helps maintain optimal inventory levels without manual intervention.

Vehicle Acquisition and Disposition

Strategic Purchasing

- **Forecast-Based Purchasing**: Purchase vehicles based on forecasted demand and market trends rather than reactive buying. Build relationships with trusted suppliers and manufacturers to secure favorable pricing and terms.
- **Trade-In Programs**: Offer attractive trade-in programs to encourage customers to upgrade their vehicles with your dealership. Properly appraise trade-in vehicles and integrate them into your inventory effectively.

Inventory Audits and Quality Control

Regular Inspections

- **Pre-Sale Inspections**: Conduct thorough vehicle inspections before listing them for sale. Ensure that each vehicle meets quality standards, address any issues promptly, and provide detailed vehicle history reports to customers.
- **Audit Procedures**: Perform regular inventory audits to verify physical inventory matches records in your DMS. Identify discrepancies, investigate root causes, and implement corrective actions to maintain data accuracy.

Environmental and Regulatory Compliance

Environmental Considerations

- **Eco-Friendly Practices**: Embrace eco-friendly practices in managing vehicle emissions, recycling materials, and reducing environmental impact associated with vehicle storage and disposal.
- **Regulatory Compliance**: Stay compliant with local, state, and federal regulations governing vehicle sales, emissions standards, safety inspections, and consumer protection laws.

Conclusion

Effective inventory management is essential for automotive dealerships to optimize profitability, enhance customer satisfaction, and maintain competitive advantage in the market. By implementing inventory planning and forecasting, efficient management practices, optimizing inventory turnover, strategic pricing and merchandising, leveraging technology, managing vehicle acquisition and disposition effectively, ensuring quality control, and complying with environmental and regulatory standards, your dealership can achieve operational excellence and sustained growth. In the next chapters, we'll explore financial management, marketing strategies, customer service excellence, leadership principles, and more—critical components for building a resilient and customer-focused automotive retail business.

Chapter 29: Customer Service Excellence in Automotive Dealerships

Welcome to Chapter 29 of your comprehensive guide on managing a successful car dealership! In this chapter, we will explore the importance of customer service excellence and provide strategies for delivering exceptional experiences to every customer who walks through your dealership doors. Customer service is not just about satisfying customers—it's about exceeding their expectations, building long-term relationships, and fostering loyalty. Whether you're interacting with first-time buyers or loyal patrons, mastering these principles will set your dealership apart in a competitive market.

The Importance of Customer Service Excellence

Building Trust and Loyalty

Customer service excellence builds trust and establishes your dealership as a reliable and customer-focused business. Positive experiences encourage repeat business, referrals, and positive word-of-mouth recommendations.

Competitive Advantage

In a competitive automotive market, superior customer service distinguishes your dealership from competitors. It becomes a key differentiator that influences customers' purchasing decisions and enhances overall satisfaction.

Creating a Customer-Centric Culture

Leadership and Training

- **Lead by Example**: As dealership leaders, embody a customer-centric mindset in all interactions. Prioritize customer satisfaction and instill these values in every team member.
- **Continuous Training**: Invest in ongoing training programs to equip your team with customer service skills, product

knowledge, and effective communication techniques. Role-play scenarios to practice handling various customer situations.

Effective Communication Skills

Active Listening

- **Listen Actively**: Pay close attention to customers' concerns, preferences, and feedback. Demonstrate empathy and understanding to build rapport and address their needs effectively.
- **Clear Communication**: Communicate information clearly and concisely, whether discussing vehicle features, pricing, financing options, or service appointments. Avoid jargon and ensure customers feel informed and confident in their decisions.

Personalized Customer Experiences

Tailoring Services

- **Individualized Approach**: Treat each customer as unique and customize your interactions accordingly. Understand their preferences, budget constraints, and vehicle requirements to offer personalized recommendations and solutions.
- **Follow-Up**: After sales or service interactions, follow up with customers to ensure satisfaction. Address any concerns promptly and show appreciation for their business.

Building Long-Term Relationships

Relationship Management

- **CRM Systems**: Utilize Customer Relationship Management (CRM) systems to maintain detailed customer profiles, track interactions, and schedule follow-ups. Use CRM data to personalize future communications and anticipate customer needs.

- **Customer Loyalty Programs**: Implement loyalty programs to reward repeat customers. Offer incentives such as discounts on service visits, exclusive events, or referral rewards to encourage loyalty and retention.

Handling Customer Concerns

Effective Resolution

- **Proactive Approach**: Anticipate potential issues and proactively address them before they escalate. Empower frontline staff to resolve complaints promptly and escalate complex issues to management when necessary.
- **Resolution Process**: Develop a structured process for handling customer complaints. Listen empathetically, apologize sincerely, propose solutions, and follow up to ensure the issue is resolved satisfactorily.

Embracing Feedback

Continuous Improvement

- **Customer Surveys**: Regularly solicit feedback through surveys or follow-up calls to gauge customer satisfaction levels. Use feedback to identify areas for improvement and implement necessary changes.
- **Feedback Analysis**: Analyze feedback trends to uncover recurring issues or opportunities for enhancement in dealership operations, customer service protocols, and overall customer experience.

Integrating Technology

Enhancing Efficiency

- **Digital Tools**: Leverage technology to streamline service appointments, vehicle inquiries, and customer communications.

Implement online scheduling systems, live chat support, and virtual vehicle tours to accommodate digital-savvy customers.
- **Customer Portals**: Offer online portals where customers can access vehicle service history, schedule appointments, and receive personalized recommendations based on their vehicle's maintenance needs.

Community Engagement and Reputation

Brand Advocacy

- **Community Involvement**: Engage with the local community through sponsorships, charity events, or partnerships. Demonstrate your dealership's commitment to social responsibility and build positive brand perception.
- **Online Reputation Management**: Monitor online reviews and social media mentions. Respond promptly to customer feedback, both positive and negative, to show transparency and commitment to customer satisfaction.

Conclusion

Delivering exceptional customer service is fundamental to the success and reputation of your automotive dealership. By fostering a customer-centric culture, enhancing communication skills, personalizing customer experiences, building long-term relationships, resolving concerns effectively, embracing feedback, integrating technology for efficiency, and engaging with the community, your dealership can cultivate loyal customers who advocate for your brand. In the next chapters, we'll explore operational excellence, leadership principles, marketing strategies, financial management, and more—essential components for building a resilient and customer-focused automotive retail business.

Conclusion: Your Road to Success in Automotive Dealership

Congratulations on completing this comprehensive guide on managing a successful car dealership! Throughout this book, we've covered essential topics ranging from business planning and financial management to marketing strategies, customer service excellence, leadership principles, and operational efficiency—all tailored specifically for automotive dealerships.

As you embark on your journey in the automotive retail industry, remember that success hinges on a combination of knowledge, dedication, and customer-centric values. By applying the principles and strategies discussed in this guide, you're well-equipped to navigate challenges, seize opportunities, and achieve your dealership's goals.

Always prioritize customer satisfaction, as it forms the bedrock of lasting relationships and business growth. Foster a team culture that values integrity, innovation, and continuous improvement. Embrace technology to streamline operations and enhance the customer experience. And above all, lead with passion, empathy, and a commitment to excellence.

As you implement these strategies, may your dealership thrive in a competitive market, earning a reputation for reliability, integrity, and exceptional service. Remember, each interaction with a customer is an opportunity to exceed expectations and create advocates for your brand.

With all my best wishes for your success,

www.ingramcontent.com/pod-product-compliance
Lightning Source LLC
Chambersburg PA
CBHW071932210526
45479CB00002B/655